We
Need
to Talk

We Need to Talk

HOW TO SUCCESSFULLY NAVIGATE CONFLICT

Dr. Linda Mintle

BakerBooks

a division of Baker Publishing Group
Grand Rapids, Michigan

© 2015 by Linda Mintle

Published by Baker Books
a division of Baker Publishing Group
P.O. Box 6287, Grand Rapids, MI 49516-6287
www.bakerbooks.com

Printed in the United States of America

Library of Congress Cataloging-in-Publication Data is on file at the Library of Congress, Washington, DC.

ISBN 978-0-8010-1676-9

Unless otherwise indicated, Scripture quotations are from the Holy Bible, New International Version®. NIV®. Copyright © 1973, 1978, 1984, 2011 by Biblica, Inc.™ Used by permission of Zondervan. All rights reserved worldwide. www.zondervan.com

Scripture quotations labeled ESV are from The Holy Bible, English Standard Version® (ESV®), copyright © 2001 by Crossway, a publishing ministry of Good News Publishers. Used by permission. All rights reserved. ESV Text Edition: 2007

Scripture quotations labeled Message are from *The Message* by Eugene H. Peterson, copyright © 1993, 1994, 1995, 2000, 2001, 2002. Used by permission of NavPress Publishing Group. All rights reserved.

Scripture quotations labeled KJV are from the King James Version of the Bible.

Scripture quotations labeled NKJV are from the New King James Version. Copyright © 1982 by Thomas Nelson, Inc. Used by permission. All rights reserved.

This book is not intended to provide therapy, counseling, clinical advice, or treatment, or to take the place of clinical advice and treatment from your personal physician or professional mental health provider. Readers are advised to consult their own qualified healthcare provider regarding mental health and medical issues. Neither the publisher nor the author takes any responsibility for any possible consequences from any treatment, action, or application of information in this book to the reader. Names, places, and identifying details have been changed to protect the privacy of individuals who may have similar experiences. The characters depicted here consist of composites of a number of people with similar issues, and the names and circumstances have been changed to protect confidentiality. Any similarity between the names and stories of individuals described in this book to individuals known to readers is purely coincidental.

In keeping with biblical principles of creation stewardship, Baker Publishing Group advocates the responsible use of our natural resources. As a member of the Green Press Initiative, our company uses recycled paper when possible. The text paper of this book is composed in part of post-consumer waste.

15   16   17   18   19   20   21   7   6   5   4   3   2   1

green press
INITIATIVE

To my many mentors in the marriage and family therapy field who taught me the benefits of confronting conflict to grow relationships. To my original family, who confronted conflict straight on but loved each other always. And to my current family who has grown and loved through confronting issues and teaching each other what it means to accept each other unconditionally.

Contents

Acknowledgments

Special thanks to:

Norm, for supporting my time and attention to writing.

Zoe, for sitting on the chair for hours while I was writing.

Dr. Jason Wells and Dr. Tony Panettiere, for checking my neuroscience.

All the couples and families I have treated over the years who helped me practically understand the role of conflict in relationships.

Wes Yoder for believing in the writing I do and encouraging me to continue.

And thanks to the Baker Books team for their work on this book and belief in my writing.

Introduction

We Need to Talk

"We need to talk . . ."
  Uh-oh, something's wrong.
  I'm in trouble.
  Oh no, not again.
  What did I do this time?
  This is going to be a long night!
  Here we go again.

It's amazing how these four short words can stop a conversation and grip us with momentary anxiety. Let's be honest, these words usually mean something is wrong and we are about to go into the world of feelings, a place not everyone likes to visit. If you are smart, you won't begin a conversation with these four words. The phrase "We need to talk" puts most of us on the defensive.

"We need to talk" takes time and energy. It can be exhausting and doesn't always end with a quick fix. But the idea behind "We need to talk" is important to making our relationships work. It's our cue that something needs to be addressed.

How do you respond to these four words? Do you embrace the idea or run for the hills? One reason this phrase makes our hearts skip a beat is because so many of us are uncomfortable working through relationship conflicts. For whatever reasons, we don't have the confidence that we can face conflict without causing more problems. And we don't like the way conflict makes us feel.

The opportunity for conflict exists moment by moment in many different forms. Think about the number of times a day we are faced with conflict. The daily news is filled with international conflicts—groups that can't get along, wars, fighting over resources, and more.

Workplace conflict is so common that consultants and special teams are often brought in to help with team building and conflict resolution. Seminars are offered to build emotional EQ, discover job fit, and understand organizational culture. Mediators work with teams to help them get along and be more productive.

Social conflict is embedded in ideologies, habits of other people, and cultures. It usually involves a struggle for power and is chronicled in stories like John Steinbeck's *The Grapes of Wrath*, the story of the hardship and oppression of migrant workers during the Great Depression, or Ralph Ellison's *Invisible Man* that takes on the segregated American South of the early part of the twentieth century and documents the struggles of being black and American.

There are physical conflicts like man against the great whale in Melville's *Moby Dick* or man struggling for survival in Daniel Defoe's *Robinson Crusoe*. In recent years, conflicts over aid distribution to survivors of hurricanes, earthquakes, and other natural disasters make global news.

Spiritual conflicts are less acknowledged but are real and related to disobedience and rebellion against God. Darkness may oppress the mind. Spiritual strongholds of ignorance, prejudice, lust, false argument, conceit, etc., may take hold.

Conflict can arise within a person as they battle personal demons like addictions and mental illness. Or it can emerge when a person acts in a manner not consistent with their beliefs, like the woman who lives with her boyfriend and believes this is morally wrong or the man who cheats on his taxes and knows this violates the law and his conscience.

Conflict is woven into our daily lives. It shows up often—in political arguments, disagreements with co-workers, fights with siblings, and marital bickering. Its consequences can bring the end of a marriage, friction between friends, or the loss of a job. Thus, this ever-present conflict can keep us stuck or it can provide growth in our relationships. To deal with conflict, we do need to talk.

We Do Need to Talk

You might as well get comfortable with the phrase "We need to talk" because all relationships have "We need to talk" moments. It is impossible to live in harmony with everyone all the time. Because of our differences, we argue and fight. But the presence of conflict does not need to make us cringe or make us think it will end poorly.

Whether conflict is over something big, like trying to decide who has child visitation, or small, like fighting over a TV remote, the way we deal with conflict matters. Conflict can move relationships forward, stall them, or even destroy them.

Conflict is difficult to handle because it involves other people, and we can't fully control other people. While that reality makes us uncomfortable and complicates things, we do control *our part* in any conflict situation. Our reactions matter when we need to talk. We focus on the part we control, not on what someone else is doing or not doing. This shift in focus is critical.

The types of conflict discussed in this book are limited to person-to-person conflict that comes from our interpersonal relationships. This type of conflict, if not handled well, can ruin relationships, create emotional instability, and tear at our very foundations of trust, security, and attachments. When conflict rules a relationship, we can't live in peace.

In the best of situations, confronting conflict brings positive results. Relief is felt once the issue is addressed. We learn more about ourselves and more about others. We see that relationships can be repaired, people can reconcile, and problems can be solved. A deeper understanding, closeness, and mutual respect can develop when we do talk.

Every Good Story Needs Conflict

In life and in fiction, every good story needs conflict. Great stories are built on the rise and fall of conflict. It is through conflict that we identify with the story's characters and emotionally invest in them. Conflict creates suspense and moves a story forward. Without conflict, there would be no tension, no drama, and no struggle between opposing forces. In fact, it is conflict that often brings people together.

Successful relationships are like successful stories. Both need conflict to grow. Since conflict is a natural part of any relationship, we do need to get comfortable with it and manage our differences in ways that value the other person. In our life stories, let's be the good guys, those who work their way through relationship problems.

Handling conflict well is a skill to be honed. It is a skill mostly learned from our original families. If we had positive role models who tackled problems and yet preserved their relationships, we were fortunate and have a solid base from which to build. If we did not have the best role models, we can learn to better equip ourselves in this important area. We aren't doomed but may need to change our ways.

We can learn to embrace conflict as a necessary part of a healthy relationship and face it with confidence. The goal, then, is not to avoid conflict or be overwhelmed by its potential intensity but to face it. Basically, we need to talk.

Like great writers who know how to resolve conflict to make a story end well, we too are writing the stories of our lives and want them to end well. The script matters as it directs the people involved in positive or negative ways. So consider this your time to work on your script and write your life with a better ending. To do so, let me ask a few questions regarding conflict:

> How do you feel when you watch or participate in conflict?
>
> Are you comfortable with the idea that conflict is a part of life?
>
> Do you avoid conflict at all costs?
>
> Do you care more about winning than about the person involved in the conflict?
>
> Do you wish you had better skills?
>
> Do you want to handle conflict in a way that is healthy, not problematic?
>
> Are you tired of being angry or upset with someone?
>
> Is there a difficult person in your life who is driving you nuts?
>
> Would you rather cut off a relationship than work through it?

If any of these questions resonate with you, this book will be an important tool in helping to make your relationships work.

Together, we'll explore the causes, the styles, the skills, and the benefits of facing our differences using relationship research, biblical instruction, and best practices in handling conflict.

We begin with three assumptions: (1) conflict is a part of all close relationships; (2) conflict, under the right conditions, can grow intimacy and bring satisfaction to relationships; and (3) in unhappy relationships, conflict escalates problems and distress and needs to be addressed.

As you read, my hope is that you will find yourself readjusting your expectations and becoming more flexible. Most of all, you will learn to approach relationships with the idea that conflict can be managed, tolerated, and handled. Finally, you will become more skillful at knowing how to promote relationship reconciliation and repair the damage we sometimes do to each other. In the end, the words "We need to talk" won't send chills down your spine or make you want to run for the hills!

1

Conflict

You Can't Get Around It

I have told you these things, so that in me you may have peace. In this world you will have trouble. But take heart! I have overcome the world.

Jesus, John 16:33

Rachel practically ran to her usual chair in my therapy office. She plopped herself down, crossed her long legs, and took a deep breath. "We need to talk," she announced as she took a quick sip from her large coffee cup. I laughed. "Isn't that what we always do when you come to my office? That is my job, you know."

She cracked a quick smile but wanted to get to it. Something was on her mind. I could tell because she was twirling her long brown curls with her finger. That was her signal to me. When Rachel talked about her mom and dad fighting, she twirled her hair. When her boyfriend pushed for more of a commitment, she twirled her hair. "I haven't told you something that happened. It's big and I have to talk to you about it."

"Okay, you've got my attention. Do I need to lie down on my couch?"

This time, she didn't smile but stared intently at that large coffee cup in her hand. Rubbing the side of the cup, she looked up and began her story.

"Something happened to me in the two weeks since I've seen you. It's great and not so great. I'm confused, which is why I need to talk. You know I have been feeling kind of empty this past year. My relationship with my parents is strained because of their constant fighting, and I'm not sure about my boyfriend. He's great in so many ways, but I just don't know, something is missing there." She continued, "So I was hanging out with a friend, talking about needing something more in my life, and she invited me to her church. You know my parents are atheists and my boyfriend doesn't have any interest in religion. But I was intrigued, and she is a really good person, so I decided to go. I can't really explain it, but in the quiet of that service, I felt God. So I gave my heart to him. Someone explained it all to me, led me through a prayer, and told me my life would change. Honestly, I felt changed. The church gave me a Bible and told me to start reading it. I did. Since then, everything is messed up. When I told my parents what happened, they laughed at me. My dad said religion is for fools. My mom believes it's just a matter of time until I come to my senses.

"Then I talked to Mark. Based on what I was reading, I didn't think I should be living with him so I told him that, and he was hurt. When I told him that I thought we should probably stop having sex, this whole faith thing didn't sit well either.

"People at the church told me my life would change. Boy, that was an understatement. My parents think I've joined a cult. I'm moving into my own place, and Mark is not happy with me. Things *have* changed. But finding God has only brought more conflict to my relationships. It's weird because I feel better inside, but outside, things aren't going so well. Please explain this to me!"

Rachel sat back, folded her hands, and waited for me to make sense of all of this.

"Rachel, that good feeling inside is God's peace. He promises peace even when things are problematic. Knowing God does not give you a ticket to escape conflict. Sometimes, like you are now experiencing, knowing God can bring more trouble because it creates conflict in your relationships.

"So when you decided to follow Christ, it went against everything your parents believe and the life you and your boyfriend were living. Even though that change is what you wanted, the people involved didn't embrace it. These differences created an opportunity for conflict.

"The way your parents and Mark want you to resolve the conflict is to stop this 'nonsense' and go back to the way things were so that nothing changes. People are comfortable with the familiar, even when the familiar is not healthy. Change is scary. Your change is uncomfortable for these people. Instead of working through these differences, they prefer to pressure you to keep things the same. This is a common reaction to change that brings conflict."

The smile returned to Rachel's face. "Thanks for the warning. And you'll help too, right?"

"That's why you pay me the big bucks! So now, how are you going to respond to your parents and boyfriend when your new life conflicts with their expectations? It's your response that matters. That's the part you control."

The conversation ended on an important note. Even though we can't always prevent conflict, we can choose how we will respond to it. We aren't victims of our pasts, circumstances, or temperaments. We can lovingly deal with people and respond in ways that promote healing, not damage.

Jesus himself addressed this with his followers when he walked the earth. In Matthew, he tells his followers that he will soon be leaving them. I'm sure they didn't want him going away, because their lives would dramatically change. But Jesus knew what was coming—that he would be denied by them, crucified, and then resurrected. He knew the conflict that was coming. And he knew they would not want him to leave.

Because of his great love and compassion for them, he warned them of the changes to come and then added, "In this world you will have trouble." The message is still true today. Expect trouble. But when we face it, we have help.

"In this world you will have trouble . . ." will probably not become your favorite Bible verse to quote. I've never seen it on a kitchen magnet! We don't want trouble. We prefer peace. We especially want peace in our personal relationships. Sometimes conflict gets in the way of that peace. However, it doesn't have to get in our way. Instead, it can be a road to change.

Conflict Is Not a Bad Thing

When most of us hear the word *conflict* we think trouble, problems, or something bad. Merriam-Webster defines conflict as a fight, a battle. It is a competitive or opposing action of incompatibility or opposing needs, drives, wishes, or external or internal demands.[1]

Relationship conflict, then, is about struggle, disagreement, argument, or debate between people. It erupts because of the way we handle different views, interests, goals, backgrounds, and expectations of those with whom we do life. When we don't handle these differences well, relationship problems result. But conflict itself is not a bad thing. It can help us grow in our relationships.

People ask, "Does there really have to be so much conflict?" The answer is yes because people are different. Every moment is a conflict opportunity. Think about it. I just woke up to begin my day. During this time, conflict can come over breakfast choices, the way I greet my spouse, what time to actually get up, who goes into the shower first, is breakfast ready on time, who is helping the kids, etc. Any of these small moments could turn to conflict because there are several people dealing with life on their own terms. Sometimes that process goes smoothly, other times it creates friction between people. When we try to do life on our own terms, like Rachel, this often conflicts with the ideas of others.

Remember, though, conflict is not a bad thing. It is normal. Expect it. Don't waste energy wishing it would go away. It won't. It is better to understand it and know how to respond. In this world, we will have trouble.

Hot-Button Conflicts

When a leading marital researcher was asked on the Anderson Cooper television show what most couples fight over, his answer made people laugh. He said that most people fight over nothing. Yes, the answer was funny, but also true. As a marital therapist, I know he is right. The subject of a fight hardly matters. What is more important is how we treat each other *during* a fight. Still, there are hot buttons that seem to set us off. These hot buttons usually include conflict over affection and sex (chapter 10), power, personality issues (chapter 11), closeness needs, social issues, and trust. And these conflicts can be fueled by stress or even a lack of knowledge.

Take Jim, for example. Jim has a short fuse when it comes to dealing with conflict. Being demoted, watching his finances dwindle, and dealing with mounting bills put him over the edge. All this stress made things worse. As a result, Jim was not an easy person to work with during this pressured time. Now, that doesn't excuse the way Jim treated his co-workers, but the outside stress certainly accentuated his already problematic conflict skills. Stress makes things worse if we aren't aware of it and allow it to manage us.

Along with stress, ignorance can make conflict worse. One wife I worked with fought constantly with her husband over the care of their young children. The wife believed a number of health-based old wives' tales about illnesses and insisted she was right even though her husband was a medical doctor. She refused to educate herself on the facts. Neither partner would compromise. She was convinced she was right, and he knew he was right! A lack of knowledge fueled this conflict. So while conflict over hot-button issues is normal, it can be worsened by stress and ignorance.

Power Struggle Conflicts

When you ask people if they want an equal relationship with others, most will answer yes. But people have widely different ideas about what *equal* means in a relationship.

Power usually relates to a person's ability to influence the other toward their own interests or goals. Power sharing means both people's needs are heard and met. Equal influence means people accommodate each other. It doesn't mean that one person is always right. And it certainly doesn't mean that one person must convince the other of their rightness!

With couples, most power struggles involve the sharing of household work, parenting, decision making, and other aspects of family life. Hurt and frustration around these issues can build when spouses *believe* all things are equal but *experience* a different reality.

Until I ask questions like, "Is each person able to express personal goals, wishes, and needs? Do you influence one another? Whose interests are shaping the relationship? Does one dominate the other? How are menial tasks like housework viewed? How are decisions made? Do both of you in a relationship feel entitled to follow your dreams, calling, or personal goals? Do you think that the source of your conflict could be related to a power imbalance?"

Jack and Amanda struggled with power imbalance. Amanda had the higher-paying job, so Jack agreed to be a stay-at-home dad. At first, Jack thought the plan was fantastic. He wanted to spend more time with his children. His dad was rarely around when he was growing up.

As the months went by, Jack felt like Amanda was taking advantage of him. She rarely helped when she got home from work, claiming she was too tired and needed downtime. Jack began to feel like money was driving this arrangement. He thought Amanda used her job to get out of sharing responsibility around the house. He also noticed that Amanda stopped asking his opinions regarding family decisions. Power was not equally shared, and Jack became resentful, insisting he return to the job market and Amanda make changes to help with the kids. The couple was at a standstill. Neither talked about the power imbalance and how they would work it out. Instead, each insisted on doing things their way. A year later, the couple divorced.

How people approach power issues impacts intimacy and relationship success. One researcher tells us that equal power is related to relationship satisfaction for both men and women. Specifically, when mutual support is shared in relationship responsibility, vulnerability, attunement, and influence, people feel good.[2] In other words, when a person feels heard, is able to influence the other, and shares responsibilities, the relationship feels more satisfying.

As two people form families, work, and develop a deeper intimacy, power struggles surface. Laura and Peter experienced this. Laura didn't mind staying home with their children until she realized that her husband, Peter, didn't value her role. His constant comments about other working wives contributing to the finances of their homes made it clear that he wanted her to work outside the home.

We know that when women's work is valued and role differences are understood and accepted, this creates fewer conflicts. This was not the case with Peter and Laura. He did not value or understand his wife's role of staying home and taking care of the kids.

Peter wouldn't directly talk about it either. Instead, he made sarcastic comments. When Laura tried to talk about the decision to stay home, he told her that she was trying to manipulate him. What Peter didn't realize was that when couples listen to each other, both genders do better with power conflicts.[3] The couple could have worked this out.

This point was driven home in a conversation I had with a young pastor recently. He was married and had two young girls. The pastor asked for my help because he was getting annoyed with his wife. She complained about how hard her job of raising the girls and keeping up with the house was, and those difficulties caused her to feel depressed. The pastor was not feeling empathy for her and said, "I know this sounds bad, but how hard could it be to take care of a house and two kids? To me, this seems like an easy job, and I don't get why she complains."

As the words left his mouth, he said, "That doesn't sound good, does it?" No, but I was glad for his honesty. He expected his wife to assume the role of housewife and mother and never complain. After all, she agreed to the job, and in his mind, it was an easy one.

If you have ever been a housewife and mother of two young kids, you know it is not an easy job. Furthermore, the job is not valued much in our culture. The pressure to be successful outside the home leaves some women feeling inadequate. This young mom needed validation from her husband. Her complaints were a bid for his attention. He was missing the point and becoming annoyed, and setting the stage for more conflict.

He didn't understand his wife or her world. He also didn't try to get her to talk about her discontent. I asked him what it would be like every day to take care of the physical needs of two young girls, not have conversations with adults, focus on menial tasks of housework, and hear the stories of friends who were in the work world and having adventures.

He thought for a moment. "I never really thought about it from her point of view."

"Maybe," I said, "she has dreams that she thinks will never happen. She has agreed to put them on hold for now, but being with the kids needs to be valued. How often do you tell her how much you appreciate her decision to be with the girls? How often do you comment on how hot she looks in those sweats and T-shirt? She's probably not feeling like the most attractive woman in the world while changing diapers and cleaning up vomit! How often do you talk to her about her dreams?"

It was like a light went on. Motherhood is often a thankless job. He took it for granted. He hadn't listened to his wife's heart or understood her needs. He had lost touch with the woman he knew before they had children. Maybe she was missing that connection with him.

The brewing conflict could be nipped in the bud if they talked about her role, if he valued her contribution to the family, and if they worked on the relationship. She needed time with him to feel like an adult again, to be refreshed and reminded of the parts of her that were not just Mommy. The tension between the two had everything to do with him not valuing her role and not seeing her as his equal partner.

You see, power inequalities undermine relationship success.[4] When power is unequal, both people are motivated to hide thoughts and emotions. The powerful one thinks they cannot be vulnerable or show weakness. This then limits communication. This is what happened to our pastor. He was the powerful one, not depressed and complaining but doing great things in the church. However, he admitted missing the intimacy with his wife as well. For months, she had hidden her thoughts until she finally started to complain. His response was to put her down and think she had no reason to complain. In his mind, she had a cake job.

Instead of telling her husband that she needed something from him (empathy, a night out, adult attention, validation), she became depressed. She did what many people do—kept it all inside, felt inadequate, and eventually started complaining. Her complaints were a bid for attention, but her husband's response was irritation, not exploration.

Complaints are often bids for more connection. They are signals that say, "Hey, something is not quite right here. Can we figure this out?" When people realize this, they can explore the problem. If they don't, complaints can turn to criticism. Later, we will see how problematic that becomes.

When another person fails to listen and minimizes the worth of the other, they become dominating and controlling.[5] The result is often jealousy, possessiveness, and excessive demands.

The less powerful one doesn't want to upset the balance and may be afraid to lose the relationship. When this is the case, the person holds back feelings, needs, and thoughts, making intimacy difficult. Conflict doesn't get addressed.

The key, then, is to minimize power imbalances. How is this done? First, pay attention to the needs and emotions of the other person. Know their inner world and respond to it. As I talked with the pastor, we explored his wife's world and identified the struggles in it. Those struggles were not silly or unimportant. To her, they represented a deeper issue—the need to be validated for a job that doesn't have immediate benefits and is often devalued in our culture.

Second, accommodate each other and balance that accommodation over time. The pastor had to make some changes. He needed to comment on his wife's work and attend to their home and kids. He also needed to get her out of the house once in a while and talk to her about her dreams. She needed to share her heart about feeling trapped and needing more of his attention. She also had to work on making peace with her homemaking decision. That was made easier by her husband's validation.

The third strategy is to share the burdens and workload of life. Many tasks are menial and not exciting but are required when two people work together. College students who share a dorm room approach menial tasks together and get them done so they can have time doing fun things. They share responsibilities and mutually support one another. This brings satisfaction.

Finally, it is important to show concern for each other's well-being. Taking the time to do a "weather" check on the other is important. A weather check is asking the other person, on a regular basis, if things are cloudy, getting a little stormy, or maybe sunny. How are we doing today? Okay? Is there anything we need to talk about?

This involves valuing that person as much as you value yourself. Share power and invest in each other. This will keep conflict at bay.

2

---◆◀---

Can We Trust Each Other?

A relationship without trust is like having a phone with no service. And what do you do with a phone with no service? You play games.

Trust is the foundation of every healthy relationship. Without trust, we cannot deal with our differences and expect things to go well. Two people, joined by family or choice, get together and hope they find a safe place to be themselves and grow. When this happens, it is easier to approach a conflict and work on the issue. You don't have to hide things when trust is present.

Trust is a process that begins in infancy and continues throughout our lives. We learn to trust through our experiences with others. Trust takes time to develop and must be nurtured in all relationships in order for them to work. That's why it's hard to trust someone you hardly know. Time is always a factor in developing trust. When you spend time with a person, you get a sense of whether or not you can trust them. Over time, they prove trustworthy or not.

Things That Erode Trust

As long as it takes to build trust, it can be broken in an instant. Whether it is a boss who promises a promotion but doesn't deliver, a friend who betrays a secret, or a pastor who uses his position to manipulate people, a lack of trust creates suspicion and brings distance to any relationship.

Secrets

I was in the grocery store yesterday, and the tabloids were head-lining the secret love child of yet another celebrity couple. Even though we tend to expect this sort of thing from celebrity relation-ships, secrets are a problem. They don't usually end well.

I am often asked if it is a good idea to reveal secrets to a partner or a friend. The answer to this begins with a question. How does it feel to find out a secret *after the fact*? For instance, do you really want to be surprised with a secret ten years into a marriage, espe-cially one that may have impacted your decision to marry in the first place? Or do you want to hear about something very personal from a stranger in a public place? Revealed secrets become gossip fodder in the wrong hands.

In my experience as a relationship therapist, keeping secrets usually backfires. Yes, secrets are difficult to bring into the light, but keeping them sets the stage for heartache down the road. The hidden thing often surfaces later. Then the reaction is even more intense because now it is associated with dishonesty. Dishonesty makes the impact worse.

Riley could attest to this. She didn't find out that she was adopted until she was an adult. In a terrible argument with her aunt, the aunt blurted out the secret. Riley was stunned and couldn't believe her parents hid this from her for her entire life. To learn the truth in an argument, from a third party, was devastating. This was not what her parents wanted to happen either, but keeping such an important secret from Riley was playing with fire. The burden of knowing the secret eventually became too much for her aunt and was blurted out in a moment of anger.

The person living with a secret carries a burden. That burden may interfere with intimacy as well. It's hard to live with secrets—the guilt, the fear, and the anxiety of being found out rarely helps a relationship. Riley's aunt hated keeping the adoption secret from her niece. She lived with the fear that she might let it slip. In a moment of anger, she did and felt deep regret. Could repairs be made? Of course, but the power of that secret led to a deeper issue of trust.

Secrets create a block in intimacy and tend to fall into three categories: (1) things that are taboo, like affairs, drug use, contracting a sexually transmitted infection; (2) a rule violation, like drinking too much at the office party, getting a speeding ticket and not telling your family, cheating on your taxes; or (3) more conventional problems, like failing a test, hiding a health problem, being dishonest about sexual partners prior to your spouse.

We keep secrets for all kinds of reasons. We may be afraid of disapproval. We may want to protect someone from hurt, or we may worry about their reaction. While you don't have to reveal every thought in your head, keeping secrets about important issues is not recommended. Self-disclosure actually helps relationships and builds intimacy.

Whom you share secrets with is important. In relationships where trust is absent, self-disclosure can open the door to betrayal, gossip, and violations of your privacy. So don't reveal your secrets to people whom you can't trust. I also don't recommend broadcasting secrets to people not involved in your affairs. There is no need for this (unless you are a public figure who has violated the trust of the public or a leader who has violated the trust of a specific group). In fact, it's better to keep those secrets between you and the person involved and those directly affected.

In our tell-all culture, where privacy is seriously lacking, discretion is needed. Be wise. Talk to the people involved in your secret, work on repair, and then carefully pray about whether or not this is something that needs to be shared with others. For example, sharing a marital secret with your entire family can be problematic. It may position family members against a spouse, even when forgiveness has been worked through and repair has been made.

Unreliability

Trust is characterized by your ability to count on someone. Is the person reliable? For example, when your mom promises to practice spelling with you and forgets, this small act begins to erode trust. When your father says he will be at your baseball game and fails to show up, trust is questioned. When your pastor says he will visit your elderly mom and never follows through, you begin to distrust him. People who aren't reliable are hard to trust.

Serena found this out. After her parents divorced, she was supposed to spend every other week with her dad. For whatever reason, he was not following through with the arrangement. As a result, Serena began to question her worth. Was she not worth her dad's time? Did he not care enough to come and get her each week? The questions and negativity were building in Serena's head. She had to talk to her dad because now she was feeling like she didn't want to be with him.

It was difficult for Serena to bring up the subject of visitation. When she did, her father made excuses. As a result of this conversation she realized that his life was full of problems that he refused to solve. His lack of follow-through had created problems in the family prior to the divorce. As much as she hated his response to her confrontation, she now knew not to expect him on weekends. Until he got help, there would be no regular visits. This was a tough loss for Serena, but she knew she couldn't control her dad. She could only grieve the loss, pray for him, and trust God to put trustworthy men in her life who made a difference.

In relationships, we build trust by showing concern for others, not simply acting on our own self-interests. That was the problem with Serena's dad. He cared more about his own interests than the interests of his daughter.

Too many times of not being there, not keeping our word, or doing something counter to what we say erodes trust and breeds conflict. One of the best ways to bring mistrust into a relationship is to act selfishly. Selfish actions say to another person, "I am not there for you." And when we feel someone is not there for us, we don't trust them.

Betrayal

In the chapter on sex and affection, I deal with sexual betrayal in detail. I don't have to convince you of how damaging and devastating sexual betrayal is to a relationship. Most of you have witnessed the heartbreak that comes with sexual betrayal with friends, family, or maybe in your own life.

Betrayal is all about broken trust, and nonsexual betrayals can be just as damaging as sexual ones. Trust is broken when someone is disloyal, lies to avoid conflict, sides against you, prioritizes work above you, and acts with disrespect or unfairness.

Kim and Jan were best friends until Kim found out that Jan betrayed her. Kim and Jan had grown up together in the church and always had each other's backs. Both went to the same small university and roomed together. When Kim shared her feelings about a young man in their biology class, she swore Jan to secrecy. She would be mortified if he found out she had a crush on him.

The two laughed about how "high school" it all sounded. Jan, in a surprising move, secretly asked this guy to go to coffee with her. She knew Kim would be upset but rationalized her actions by telling herself that it was an innocent request to get to know this man. But in Jan's heart, she was tired of Kim always winning the dates and getting the guy. This time, she would make a move, even though she knew her best friend trusted her with her feelings.

She went for coffee, flirted, and was asked out on a date. She still didn't tell Kim and continued to listen to Kim talk about her growing attraction to this guy. Kim even asked Jan for advice on how to get him to notice her. Jan grew more and more uncomfortable with her secret relationship until one day Kim noticed a text message from the guy on Jan's cell phone.

"Why is he texting you?" Kim asked. "I thought you didn't know him. All this time you've been lying to me? Never telling me you were dating him? What kind of a friend does that?"

Kim was deeply hurt, and Jan knew she had betrayed her best friend over a guy. The two were able to talk through the problem, but their relationship changed. Kim, who thought she knew Jan well, couldn't believe Jan would do what she did. And Jan, who knew Kim well, never thought she would feel jealous of her best friend. The betrayal proved to be a wedge in their relationship. The next semester, the two decided to find new roommates and get some space away from each other. Kim told me the relationship never returned to the same intimacy.

How to Build Trust

When trust is eroded or falls apart, it sets the stage for mistrust. Mistrust can lead to loneliness and isolation. We withdraw from people who let us down and live with disappointment if we don't choose to confront their actions. We don't want to talk to people we can't trust. Why should we bare our souls or be vulnerable with people who will use our transparency to their advantage? But if we don't confront the mistrust, there is no opportunity to grow or work through the problem.

How do you go about building trust with someone you've hurt? The key is to know the other person's world and reliably respond to it. Do what you say. Keep your promises. Empathize with the other person's issue and try to see the problem from both sides.

Serena's dad needed to see the failed visits from his daughter's point of view. He let her down. She needed him. He could change this if he would take responsibility.

When differences emerge and pain is associated with those differences, don't dismiss the pain. Acknowledge it, empathize, and be there for that person. This is how you create a safe haven to work through differences.

When differences are expressed and that expression is negative, stay calm and listen to those feelings. Do not get defensive, turn away, or decide to avoid or make excuses. Stay in it. The person who has the conflict is trying to connect with you. When you stay in the conflict, trust builds. The person learns that they can have issues and that you will stay in the relationship and work through those issues with them. This is what creates safety and a secure attachment.

An important part in building trust is not turning conflict into a win-lose argument or debate. *American Idol*'s Randy Jackson's sentiment "He's in it to win it" doesn't fly with conflict. Disagreements aren't about winning; they are about understanding. We aren't in conflict to win it. Our aim is to understand the other, consider our part, and take responsibility where necessary. This is what creates a win-win outcome.

Finally, when trust is broken, repair is needed. Repair begins with forgiveness. Forgiveness is so important that it has its own chapter. In my opinion, people deserve a second chance and a right to win back trust. We all make mistakes and need a little grace in our lives.

The Importance of Second Chances and Boundaries

When your trust is violated, check your thinking. It may become quite negative. When trust is breached, it is easy to allow negative thoughts toward that person to multiply. People get angry when trust is broken. This is normal. But it's what you do with your anger that counts. You can feel it, label it, and acknowledge it, but holding on to it ends in resentment.

To guard against such negativity, give the offender the benefit of the doubt. Everyone makes mistakes. It is not necessarily a character flaw for someone to let us down or breach our trust. Mistakes can be talked about and figured out so that they do not recur. People in committed relationships try again, believing that trust can be rebuilt.

Now, if a person repeatedly shows you that they are not trustworthy, then boundaries are needed. Even so, continue to forgive, but you don't have to put yourself in harm's way. Whitney learned this.

Everyone told Whitney that her boyfriend was like her father. Neither of them was reliable when it came to showing up for events. Whitney's dad was notorious for promising to come to Whitney's performances, but rarely did he follow through. He always apologized and said he would do better. He didn't.

Whitney dated Ryan, who managed to do the same thing. He would promise to meet her somewhere and not show up. Whitney justified this behavior by telling herself that Ryan was immature and needed to grow up. She always came up with a reason for his failure to be true to his word.

Whitney's friends felt differently. They thought it was mean of Ryan to promise to meet her somewhere and not call or show up, immaturity or not. To Whitney's friends, this was a sign that Ryan could not be trusted, and they pushed her to confront Ryan. Whitney didn't because she believed it would cause a fight and that Ryan might break up with her. Then she would be alone. That possibility scared her more than the lack of follow-through.

Each time Ryan no-showed, he, like her dad, promised to do better but never changed his behavior. Each time he apologized, Whitney forgave him. But Whitney began to notice other small things that Ryan failed to do. In her heart, she knew Ryan could not be trusted and that she had found a man just like her father.

She finally realized that the heartache of disappointment would be with her for a long time if she didn't confront the problem. So with the encouragement of her friends, Whitney confronted Ryan on his broken promises. She told him she could no longer date him if he continued in this way. Whitney had to set a boundary and show self-respect. Ryan promised to do better but in the end proved he wasn't reliable. Eventually, Whitney summoned her courage and broke off the relationship. When she did, she felt relieved. She knew she didn't want a second unreliable man in her life. Yes, she continued to forgive her father, but she knew she could never depend on him. That was sad, and a loss she had to grieve. But with her choice of a partner, she could wait for someone who would be true to his word. She did not have to repeat the family pattern. Some people just blow it, are repentant, and get back on track. Others may want to change and have a difficult time making the turn and need professional help. Still others are repeat offenders, and it is part of their character to be unreliable. These people don't learn from their mistakes and refuse to take responsibility. These are the people needing boundaries.

In Whitney's case, she didn't assume Ryan's unreliability was a character flaw. It turned out, however, that it was. But she began by giving him the benefit of the doubt and did not allow the first time he broke his promise to dissuade her in the relationship.

In most cases, when trust has been breached, it is worth a try to repair. Stay positive. If it looks like the person is unwilling or unrepentant, be realistic. Not all breaches of trust can be repaired because repair requires both people to make an effort. Yet, many times people are willing to try. Give the person a chance. Remember, trying to work through conflict helps you develop those skills and brings growth. Walking away does neither.

Jesus as Our Model

Jesus knew the heartbreak of betrayal when he watched his beloved disciples turn against him. Judas gave him over to his enemies for money. Peter denied him for fear of retaliation. Yet Jesus in his mercy and grace chose to forgive. The betrayers didn't deserve it, but that was the point. Grace gives what isn't deserved. It's not about being right; it's about doing right!

Jesus's claim to be the Messiah caused conflict. Not everyone believed his claim. In fact, some people called his claim heresy and plotted to kill him. Jesus knew who he was despite the accusations. He refused to allow the betrayers to deter him.

Jesus could fight back. He could prove he was right. At his disposal were ten thousand angels ready to rescue him from a death he did not deserve. He could get angry, call foul play, retaliate, and seek revenge.

Who could blame him if he reacted this way? Jesus was, after all, also fully man. Tempted to do what we are tempted to do. Prove ourselves right. Would he put an end to those who wrongfully accused him or *do* right and reconcile man to God? Would he show tolerance and restraint in the face of provocation? His response would determine our future.

No angels or armies were called from heaven. The decision to *do* right ended in dying alone. There he was, wounded for our transgressions, bruised for our iniquities, and the chastisement of our peace was upon him, meaning the punishment that brought us peace was on him. Because of his response, our reconciliation to God is now possible.

We tell ourselves it is more important to be right than to do what is right. Jesus says that is backward. Don't sacrifice your relationship to be right. *Do* what is right. To do right means to try to reconcile our conflicts with others, even when things are unfair. Sometimes this is easy, but most times this is hard. It's much easier to walk away and be right than stay in the relationship and tolerate betrayal.

If we listen to the sermon Jesus gave on the mount, we hear the high premium he placed on doing right. He told us to work out our differences and do it in a way that preserves our relationships. Be reconciled one to another: "Blessed are the peacemakers, for they will be called children of God" (Matt. 5:9). Don't carry malice in your heart. Rather, give forbearance for retaliation, forgiveness for wrongs, and restoration of fellowship. Those are strong words from our Lord, but he modeled the way.

3

I'd Rather Not Talk

The web of our life is of a mingled yarn, good and ill together.

William Shakespeare

What if I don't want to talk? If my mother-in-law is driving me crazy, can't I just ignore her? Or, if I get too upset talking to my ex over visitation, can't I just ignore him?

Obviously, we can choose to ignore conflict and make it through life. People do it all the time. For example, your mother-daughter relationship won't fall apart if you ignore conflict with her once in a while. But a pattern of ignoring conflict can hurt relationships. Avoiding is not a good way to grow your relationships. The "I'd rather not talk" attitude may work in the moment but not in the long run.

Avoidance and Your Physical Health

Avoiding conflict does initially reduce stress. The problem is that avoidance builds tension. A number of studies point to physical problems when people choose to avoid conflict. One study noted that while people feel better avoiding at the time of a conflict, they don't feel better the next day. In the study, physical symptoms and negative well-being increased the day *after* the conflict when people chose to avoid rather than confront problems.[1] In other words, you pay the next day.

Mallory found this out. Mallory was angry with her friend Victoria for overstepping a boundary with her boyfriend. Instead of going to Victoria, Mallory was building resentment. The thought of confronting Victoria made Mallory anxious. She knew Victoria would not handle the confrontation well and would be mad at her. Mallory didn't want to engage in the drama.

Temporarily, Mallory delayed the stress of a confrontation. But day after day, her stomach hurt, and frustration with her friend was building. The anxiety was causing sleep problems. She knew she had to talk to Victoria.

Like so many times in our lives, we may opt for a short-term benefit but then reap a negative consequence later. Take overeating, for example. The food tastes good at the moment, is even enjoyable, but the weight gain that comes later is the price we pay. The same is true of conflict. We pay a price when we ignore it. That price may even be a shorter life.

In another study, researchers at the University of Michigan looked at conflict as it relates to longevity of life. They found that people who deal with conflict live longer. Specifically, they observed that when both partners in a relationship felt unfairly attacked and suppressed their anger at the other, they died earlier than couples who communicated their anger.[2]

There is an exception, a time when avoiding conflict might be best. This involves confronting someone who can physically harm you. When someone is so angry and cannot calm down, and you are at risk for a physical altercation or explosion, do not confront. You can't deal with conflict, nor should you, when someone is physically threatening or unable to get control of their emotions.

At those times, the parties need to wait until they are able to calm down and it is safe to confront. Even then, safety may be questionable if there is a history of out-of-control anger.

Certain personality types make confrontation more difficult. Some people have high-conflict personalities. Strategies for handling differences with high-conflict people will be discussed in chapter 11.

Rocking the Boat

Often we avoid talking about problems because we prefer not to rock the relationship boat. Conflict requires us to take a position and assert our views or opinions. If we are afraid or unsure of what we think or believe, we may decide not to deal with an issue. Even when we know what we want, we have to listen to the other person and try to navigate a solution. This takes a lot of work and can be exhausting.

At times, the stress of our lives depletes our energy to deal with relationship problems. I see this regularly as a family therapist. Take the Smith family, for example. They are dealing with a drug-addicted twenty-year-old. The number of times this young adult has been in and out of treatment has left the family drained emotionally and financially. The addiction is still raging, confrontation is still needed, but the family is growing weary. At times, they feel like giving up but know they can't. They must stay in the fight and continue to respond in ways that are not enabling. This takes time and perseverance.

One family member had a dream in which the drug addiction was gone, her brother restored, and the family happy again. All the stress from the tension of holding firm boundaries with her brother was gone. She longed for that day because the constant turmoil exhausted her and was zapping any joy from her family. Family therapy was working, but the energy it took to assert herself and deal with her brother was draining.

No one would disagree. But conflict avoidance was a major factor that contributed to her brother's addiction. The family pattern had to change in order to support his sobriety. That change required confronting difficult issues that brought up pain. In the end, the perseverance to stay in the game paid off.

When we care about people, we need to decide if avoiding conflict in order to reduce immediate stress is better than mustering the energy and courage to confront problems and improve the relationship in the long run. One reason this is such a difficult decision is that we don't like to feel the tension that comes with confrontation. It is uncomfortable.

Lisa's family almost succumbed to this discomfort. Lisa's parents suspected she was struggling with an eating disorder. They noticed Lisa pushing food around her plate to make it look like she was eating. They saw her food selections dwindle to salads and low-fat items. And they grew increasingly concerned about Lisa's continuing weight loss. Lisa's mom said something to Lisa about what she saw, but Lisa insisted her mom was overly concerned.

Denial can be a strong wall to push against. When Lisa's parents asked me what to do, I told them to confront Lisa again. But I prepared them for her reaction. She would again be upset, would question their parenting and trust in her, and would minimize the symptoms. They needed to hold a firm line for her to get help no matter how upset she became. It helped the family to know that a negative reaction to the confrontation of an eating disorder is normal. However, once the person engages in therapy, they are usually the first to say the confrontation was necessary. In the end, they thank the confronters for not backing off. It usually saves their lives!

Confrontation with adults is like parenting kids. The kids don't always like it when you hold them accountable, but you do it for their good. In the end, they are better people for it, and they may even thank you. You can't parent well and never rock the boat. The same is true of most relationships—boat rocking is often necessary to move the boat forward.

Eruptions and Backlog

Sometimes avoidance of conflict can lead to explosions and sudden eruptions when there is a backlog of pent-up feelings. Explosive emotions often feel like they are coming from nowhere. Someone says something innocuous, and suddenly the other person explodes. It doesn't make sense unless the person is reacting to things that have built up over time. When the explosion feels too big for the issue at hand, something is usually brewing under the surface. When this happens, conflict feels scary and out of control. This feeling reinforces avoidance.

Other times, conflict simmers below the surface, creating irritability. This was Derek's problem. Growing up, he was the recipient of humiliation from his dad whenever he disagreed. Consequently, Derek learned to avoid conflict in order to not be humiliated. He carried this pattern into his workplace. As a result, he found himself irritable and snapping at small things. This was creating problems with his co-workers. The last thing Derek wanted was to be humiliated by a boss or colleague (even though he had no history of this happening), so he chose to avoid issues. As we know, a simmering pot eventually boils!

Even when there isn't a backlog of unresolved conflict, some people avoid it because they are afraid they will become out of control or the other person will lose control. Again, in families where anger isn't handled well, conflict can be frightening.

In order to create safety in relationships, people have to commit to controlling their anger. Calming down is an essential skill for relationships to work. More will be said about this later in the chapter on anger.

In addition, there are conflict skills that work to repair relationship damage quickly and keep a relationship strong. Those skills are presented later as well. For now, you might not want to talk, but think about pushing yourself to do it. You can avoid buildup and explosions if you deal with issues when they present themselves.

Grace Notes

Sometimes, because we don't want to talk, we may miss the opportunity to resolve a conflict. Sharon's story, sadly, is an example of this. Sharon and her mom were estranged for years over differences in lifestyle. Neither would give in enough to begin a conversation to reconcile. Tragically, Sharon's mom was hit by a drunk driver and instantly killed. Sharon never had the opportunity to work through her differences with her mom and reconcile their relationship.

Sharon came to therapy a mess. Guilt gripped her life, and she knew the recent feelings of depression were created by the unfinished business with her mom. The opportunity to work through these issues was gone. Now, she had to find a way to forgive herself and live with the unresolved issues. This meant grieving what did not happen and letting go of the loss. Her mother-daughter relationship could not be repaired, but she could lose the guilt and depression associated with it.

Sometimes, as in Sharon's case, we have to make peace with our decisions, knowing we didn't make the best ones. Thankfully, there is grace! Grace is what brings hope and healing. Because of grace, we can accept our failures and learn from our mistakes.

As a musician, I am familiar with grace notes. They are often written into the scores of music. The grace note is smaller than the regular note. Usually there is a slash through the note stem, and the grace note is placed just before the main note to be played. Grace notes help accentuate the main note, but they are quick and fleeting to the main melody.

But God's grace is the main note and is not quick and fleeting. Grace is God's unmerited favor toward us. His grace allows us to let go of bad decisions.

When we fall short, Scripture tells us his grace is sufficient, meaning he knows our need and will strengthen and comfort us. When we are weak in ourselves, God is strong in us. Because of his grace, we don't have to live with guilt.

After her mom's death, Sharon vowed not to let unresolved conflict linger in her life anymore. No matter how uncomfortable it made her, she would tackle a relationship problem as best she could. In the meantime, we focused on the good memories she had with her mom. Those good memories helped her see that her relationship was not all bad; only parts of it were problematic.

Even with Sharon's willingness to look at her past and current relationships, accepting God's grace in this situation was the key to her healing. Now she could do things differently and learn from her mistakes.

Sharon would urge each of us to try to work out relationship conflicts as soon as possible. She would say, don't wait because we don't know what tomorrow brings. The biblical prescription to not let the sun go down on your anger is wisdom. Whenever possible, resolve issues as soon as possible, don't avoid them. Even if the issue can't be resolved, you can rest assured that you tried and you can allow God's grace to work in the situation. And if you missed the opportunity, accept God's grace and move forward.

4

Differences Make a Difference

It is not our differences that divide us. It is our inability to recognize, accept, and celebrate those differences.

Audre Lorde

When Kim Kardashian dyed her hair blonde after the birth of her first child, she made national news. Why would Kim dye her hair? Do more people prefer blondes to brunettes? Do blondes really have more fun? Why would anyone care? It's only hair color, people!

Apparently, people do care. Rose-Marie Jarvis of Goody Hair conducted a survey of over 3,000 participants and found that blondes engage in their beauty routines an average of 72 minutes a day, 6 minutes longer than brunettes. This means blondes spend 22 days a year getting ready, compared to 19 days for those lagging-behind brunettes. The reason: blondes have to work harder to get that same light hair shine that brunettes already possess. Yet, all that extra time spent getting ready makes blondes feel more con-fident, leading to more fun![1]

The survey also found that blond men tend to like blonde women, and brunette men prefer brunette women. When it comes to attraction and hair color, people look for similarity. This is also true in many other aspects of relationships. We are drawn to those with similar characteristics. In other words, like attracts like.

The preferences we develop are also often born out of our experiences. If you socialized with a certain hair-color type growing up and had good experiences with that hair type, you will be attracted to that hair color as an adult. But say the blond bully picked on you in middle school. You probably won't be attracted to the blond drummer in the band. He is too much of a negative childhood reminder.

These perceptions influence our views of how we think of people. Overall, blondes are perceived to be more attractive and even do better at getting tips as waitresses.[2] When brunettes first meet other people, they are perceived as being smarter than blondes. (Think of all the "dumb blonde" jokes and how those jokes affect perceptions.) But even though brunettes are perceived to be smarter, blondes go on more dates and feel more confident and youthful.

Something like hair color is a preference influenced by experiences and perceptions. It is not a need. Ms. Kardashian didn't *need* to change her hair color. Preferences make us happy when they are fulfilled, but they typically don't create serious dissatisfaction in our lives when they aren't met. However, if we don't realize that a preference is simply our feeling of liking something more than something else, we can create unnecessary conflict and bad feelings.

For example, my preference is to have a small dog. This is not a need. Small dogs make me happy, but not getting my preference isn't going to lead me to depression. What if I found a big dog that needed a home? What if my neighbor has a big dog that I adore? Or what if my spouse prefers a big hunting dog? The two of us have different preferences when it comes to dogs. It's not a question of right or wrong.

The game changes, however, if we insist that our preferences are right and we need others to agree with us. For example, if Kim Kardashian's significant other insisted she change her hair color because he prefers blondes, this could create conflict. When someone demands that we like what they like, then we need to talk.

As long as we don't confuse preferences with need, we can keep conflict to a minimum. So if you are fighting over a TV show, which store to go to next, or what type of meat to buy, ask yourself if this conflict is about a need or a preference? If it is only a preference, is it worth fighting over? Or is this one of those times to flip a coin or accommodate the other person?

Reacting to Preferences and Differences

In the blogosphere, people don't hold back on their reactions to preferences or differences. Maybe it is because they can be anonymous. It takes thick skin to handle the unkind comments that come with sharing your thoughts, positions, and opinions. Most people are kind and considerate, but there are those who feel it is their job to take you down with insults.

For example, when Madonna was the Super Bowl halftime entertainment in 2012, I blogged on my BeliefNet blog, *Doing Life Together*, that I wasn't impressed with her show and thought a different choice of entertainer would have been better. I blogged,

A friend of mine asked me who still listens to Madonna? I really don't know. She must sell music or she wouldn't have been asked to do this gig. But every time I see Madonna, I feel like I am seeing a little girl locked in a grown-up body. She seems like a wounded soul who is desperately seeking someone other than Susan!

And maybe that is what I sense—the seeker searching for validation and acceptance. I suspect that under all the bravado and strutting is a woman in need of someone to love and to be loved back. She's tried spirituality, but needs the love of Jesus.

The blog went on to say that watching her perform was uncomfortable, like watching a former beauty queen trying to regain her title. In my *opinion*, older rock stars can still perform, but there is something unsettling about watching them at fifty years of age trying to be twenty.

I didn't think what I said was controversial at all. I was doing my job, what I get paid to do—sharing an opinion and opening the door for other people to agree or disagree.

My opinion triggered over-the-top reactions in some people. Rather than tolerate a difference in preference, they personally attacked me. I got hate mail from the Madonna post. People told me I was ugly and jealous, called me names, accused me of being judgmental (I'm supposed to give an opinion), and more—all over an opinion that I preferred a different entertainer for reasons I outlined. A few people were so over the top, I had to remind them to comment within the rules of conduct as outlined by the blog site. The intensity of anger targeted at me for my opinion made me wonder what I was triggering in the readers' personal lives.

People in relationships usually clash over differences far more important than entertainer preferences. It is those differences in perceptions, beliefs, values, temperaments, family background, expectations, and more that cause upset and lead to problems.

In healthy relationships, we tolerate differences in preferences. In unhealthy relationships, we don't. Fighting about preferences is a waste of time. Save conflict for more meaningful differences.

Moving beyond Preferences

Differences are a fact of life and often can bring many positives to our world. For instance, the extrovert pursues the introvert because they see things in that person that are missing in the self. It's as if we unconsciously try to complete ourselves by finding those missing parts in others. This means we are also attracted to differences, especially those differences that feel like they complete us or provide something we are missing.

But when we try to change people to be like us, differences can be dividing and problematic. Conflict is often an outcome of trying to dominate or control another. Then those differences that attracted you to someone can pull you apart.

Rather than skillfully working through our differences, most of us reluctantly accommodate each other, sometimes manipulate and coerce the other, or live in la-la land and pretend conflict doesn't exist. Differences can prove quite challenging.

On the plus side, friction can help motivate us to explore our differences, learn about ourselves and others, and work things out. The working out involves talking about differences respectfully and with appreciation. The key is to be open and accepting in order to learn from each other. We'll learn about the importance of navigating and negotiating these differences in the rest of this chapter.

Clarifying Expectations

Conflict develops in relationships directly related to our expectations of the other person. Unconsciously, we want the other person to change to fit some idealistic view we have. For example, we want our mother to be all-caring and meet every need. Or we think our partner can do no wrong initially. This idealizing causes tension because people can't live up to the unrealistic expectations we hold.

In love, for example, we soon discover that our partner cannot meet all our needs all the time. Our expectations must be modified to a more realistic level or disappointment sets in. No person, no matter how wonderful he or she is, will respond to you exactly like you need every time. People let us down because they are not perfect!

For example, when Misty and Ashton were dating, Ashton was very attentive to Misty's needs. Now that they are married, Ashton's attentiveness has diminished. Misty feels either he has changed or he isn't the person she thought he was. She is disappointed because she expected more.

The more she knows Ashton, the more she realizes she didn't take enough time to really get to know him before they married. And she didn't talk about expectations before the marriage. Learning about a partner's expectations and being up front with our own takes time, but the effort is well worth it.

Realize the Differences between Men and Women

I don't remember getting any instruction on how to deal with differences when I got married. Here was this man, similar to me in values but very different in terms of how he approached life. Our expectations for independence, interdependence, and togetherness were quite different and took us years to sort out. Along the way, we had lots of "we need to talk" moments.

I did what most people do—tried to change my partner to be more like me. Most of us know this does not work. Yet we seem determined to try.

What I didn't know then was that men and women often speak a different language. Consider this example. Craig and Kirsten are out to dinner. Kirsten begins the conversation.

"How was your day?"

"Fine."

That's it. Craig stops talking, and Kirsten is frustrated. Kirsten is thinking that a little more detail would be nice.

If Kirsten talked about her day, it might go more like this:

"I had a crazy day at the office. Joyce got mad at our boss and lost it. Everyone was upset but afraid to say anything. It was a nightmare. What was your day like?"

"Actually good."

The men reading this are thinking, good grief, too much information! But are Craig and Kirsten's answers a function of the different social behaviors of men and women?

Studies have shown that the differences in men's and women's brains are more of a matter of degree, not of kind, meaning the two genders are more alike than different. A study at the University of Pennsylvania says that the brain wiring in men and women may account for this difference in degree. According to the researchers, gender differences in brain wiring begin to be seen in adolescence. Images of male brains show more connections *within* hemispheres. Women's brains show more *between* hemispheres.[3]

This means that women are more suited to multitasking and analytical thought; they express themselves using emotional states and are more socialized toward emotions from an early age. Yes, men, this might be why you find us overwhelming at times. Men are better at linear tasks that require attending to one thing at a time. They too feel things deeply but don't process things as quickly as women or put those feelings into words.

Furthermore, when an argument happens, women may stay upset longer. This is possibly due to the enhancing effects of estrogen that can prolong the secretion of the stress hormone. So when a man says, "Let it go, get over it," he already has!

We know that sharing emotions does help relationships. So men, take a deep breath and think about what you might be feeling. Ladies, don't ask men "to talk" when they are watching football or fixing the sink. When you do talk, edit your speech and tell him what you need. Men, pay attention to your physical body and verbalize what you are feeling. Share a few more thoughts than a one-word answer. In other words, let's become more fluent in each other's language.

Identify Role Expectations

Role expectations are also important to discuss and negotiate. Role expectations are those expectations we carry around about specific roles we have like mother, father, daughter, working person, etc. If these role expectations are not clarified and negotiated, people can become stressed, depressed, or lose self-esteem.

For example, a woman's expectation of being a good mother may include staying home with young children, but if her husband expects her to work outside the home and contribute financially, this difference in role expectations can cause conflict. Again, it is not about one person being right or wrong but about how those different role expectations are handled.

Identify Unspoken Expectations

Expectations are like maps used to navigate the road of our perceptions. We all have expectations, but we do not always share them in our relationships. Instead we assume people will act in certain ways or that people should know our expectations without us having to tell them. But when the expectations are unspoken, there is no map for the other person to follow. We may feel hurt, angry, or betrayed that they aren't fulfilling our expectations, when they don't even know what those expectations are!

When expectations are unknown, it may take conflict to bring them out into the open. This was the case with Sam and Tara. They had a wedding date but wondered about their compatibility. Planning the wedding highlighted a number of differences including how to spend money.

Sam's family expected a simple ceremony, given the couple was still paying off student loans and just beginning their careers. They really couldn't afford an elaborate wedding. If Sam and Tara couldn't pay for the wedding they wanted, Sam's family believed they should scale down rather than take out loans. Sam's dad had never been in debt and owed nothing to the bank. His approach to money was you don't spend what you don't have.

Tara was the only girl in her family and had always dreamed of a lavish wedding. She thought it would be worth the debt to create an experience she and Sam would remember for the rest of their lives. Tara's family was comfortable with taking out loans and accumulating debt. Tara's father had operated his various businesses in the red but had always managed to make their finances work. He believed in borrowing and taking out loans to build a dream.

The different money approaches were creating conflict between the two families. Sam and Tara had different expectations as to how to approach the wedding based on their beliefs about money. They weren't sure what to do and had been unable to get everyone to agree to a plan. Is one family right? Are they both right? Or is it even about being right?

In Sam and Tara's case, finances and expectations needed to be discussed and brought out into the open. Once the couple understood the two different approaches to finances, they could negotiate a solution.

Identify Different Values and Beliefs

We all have certain convictions we hold to be true. Usually these convictions are tied to religion or some worldview or philosophy. For example, Christianity asserts we are sinners in need of a Savior. A secular humanist would have a different view, believing in the goodness of man and denying the supernatural. Families, culture, media, and experience shape our beliefs as well. Our assumptions and beliefs about life inform our thoughts, actions, and emotions.

Values come from beliefs. They are what we believe to be important and govern how we behave and interact with others. Values are tied to our priorities and serve as the basis for making decisions. For example, if a man values his family, he takes time to be with them. Values are more amenable to change because they are based on what we believe to be true. Our beliefs can change too.

Values and beliefs both play into relationships. Let's say you believe a dating couple should treat each other with respect. In your relationship, you will be happy or satisfied when your partner respects you. But, let's say your girlfriend doesn't share this belief. She grew up with a mother who constantly disrespected her father and believes that men are not necessary to have around. Her belief feeds her devaluing of men, thus, she is okay disrespecting them.

Negotiating Our Expectations

When an expectation is violated by an event or action, defenses are activated. We may deny a problem because it isn't consistent with our view of the person. Or we may punish the person for not meeting our expectations. However, this only perpetuates the very things we complain about.

Or we may reinforce behaviors that fit our expectations of what we want to see, hoping this will increase the likelihood the person will stay within our expectations.

Let's say your wife takes a long time to get ready for a dinner with the boss. Being on time is an expectation you have. You are running late and your frustration is growing. "Honey, I know we want to make a good impression on the boss and not be late, so we need to get going. Are you almost ready? If not, how can I help?"

If you get upset because your partner is regularly late for dinner, address the issue. First, share your expectation of a call, notice, or some courtesy regarding the lateness. Then begin asking questions about why this continues to happen. Even say, "I don't want to assume the wrong idea, but without you telling me what is going on, I [fill in the blank]."

Once you share expectations and discuss the reasons for the lateness, negotiate a solution. Concentrate on what can be changed to better meet both of your needs. The purpose of doing this is to prevent disillusionment and growing negativity, both precursors to divorce.

An important tool in negotiating expectations is to check our assumptions. Instead of assuming that the intentions of the other person are negative, we can assume good intentions and do some checking, which can calm down a situation. A more positive interpretation of a person's motivation creates goodwill between two people and builds positivity. The reverse is also true. Negative assumptions about a person build negativity in the relationship.

Learning from Our Original Families

An important part of counseling is helping people understand that conflict emerges from the different backgrounds and expectations two people bring to a relationship. We all grow up in unique families that have their own ways of doing things. When two people come together in a relationship, those unique ways have to be negotiated and accommodated or conflict arises.

I'm sure you can think of both small and big differences in your current relationships that came from your family backgrounds. Here is one that comes to mind from mine. I grew up in a family that always had a live Christmas tree during the Christmas season. Part of the fun was going to a lot, picking out the tree, and hauling it home. The smell of the fresh evergreen filled the living room and was part of our tradition. Warm memories are associated with the live tree, a reminder of days gone by with special loved ones.

My husband had a very different experience growing up. He spent many holidays on the mission field in the country of Honduras. There were no live evergreens. His tree was a fake silver tree that you assemble. On the mission field, you make do with whatever you can. In the absence of fields of pine trees, his family did their best to celebrate.

To my husband, putting up a real tree means a lot of work. We have to spend time looking for just the right tree, tie it up on the car, set it up, string the lights, and then decorate. If we had a fake tree, we would simply bring it up from the basement, zip it out of its bag, and voila, the tree!

Every year we talk about whether we should get a fake or real tree. I hate the idea of a fake tree, and my husband thinks it would be great. Through the years, my husband has conceded to my desire for a real tree. Now, with our children in college, he is pushing hard for a fake tree. The work involved in getting the tree, setting it up, lighting and decorating it is not worth it in his mind. (Men, stop nodding your heads!)

This difference has created a conflict. Thankfully, that conflict hasn't led to a major problem yet because he does not feel strongly enough to fight for his preference. Yes, accommodation is a helpful character trait when it comes to couples dealing with conflict. But the future is uncertain.

I can tell you that over the years when my mom would make a request like having a real tree, my dad usually accommodated her. So my husband doing the same works for me! But if he decides not to accommodate my request in the future, how we handle this conflict will be important. Not because the tree is an important subject in our family life, but because our family patterns influence how we behave.

Take Tim, for example. During a session one day, he said to me, "You really don't expect me to bring up that issue to my friend. He'll probably stop talking to me."

"What's the alternative? You live with this secret and allow it to eat away at you? Do you want that? Or can you trust that he will understand? He may not like what you did, but telling him might make things better in the long run. Right now, you are stuck because you feel bad and can't shake your guilty conscience. If you decide to tell him, we can practice how to do that. The way you talk about the problem is important, and I can walk you through it. Your fear is that he will stop being your friend, but nothing in your relationship indicates he will do that. In the past, he has shown you that honesty is better than secrets."

Tim wasn't convinced. He came from a family that didn't handle conflict well. In fact, any time his mom tried to tell his dad how she really felt, his dad blew up and left the room. In Tim's experience, conflict meant being left or abandoned. Tim had an expectation that dealing with conflict in a relationship would result in bad things. That expectation was causing problems. His friend Daniel repeatedly told Tim to tell him if something was wrong.

Daniel had a very different experience growing up. His family encouraged each other to bring up issues. In fact, his dad always said, "Best to get things out in the open so we can deal with them. Otherwise, you feel the tension but don't know why." Daniel's approach to conflict was to deal with it directly. He wanted to know if a problem was brewing. He was confident that conflict could be worked through. His expectation was that dealing with conflict ends in stronger friendships.

Both Tim and Daniel were approaching conflict based on early experiences with parents. Their ideas about conflict were learned from their families and were now influencing their friendship.

If you grew up in a home where conflict was avoided at all costs, you probably bring that pattern to your relationships. If you marry someone who is used to confronting conflict because that is how people solved problems in their family growing up, these learned patterns may or may not be compatible with each other.

The danger comes when we think our way is the right way. The truth is that in most cases, one person isn't right or wrong, just different. In the tree example, I can feel passionate about a live tree, but that doesn't make me right. My commitment to my position is based on my past experience—what evokes great memories and meaning—not on some factual truth.

This is why it is important to talk about our family backgrounds and experiences. It is how we understand each other better. In fact, one of the places I begin in counseling is to ask about family patterns.

How do people in your family deal with anger? How was conflict handled? What happened when people disagreed about anything? When stress was high, how did people in your family cope? These and other questions are designed to help me and the other person better understand what they bring to the relationship from their original families. Sometimes, just knowing the differences helps. Other times, we have to work on accommodating and negotiating these differences.

A simple exercise for you and someone you care about is to list and talk about how things were handled in your original families. Then talk about the differences. Identify points of potential conflict. Go a little deeper and see if you can talk about the meaning attached to certain ways of doing things. It is the meaning attached to our positions that creates emotion. If we fail to understand the meaning, we can grow apart.

For example, Dave realized that his father yelled when he argued with his mom. He noticed he was doing the same with his wife. When he and his wife had arguments, he felt overwhelmed physically and yelled to release tension. He realized that yelling was his attempt to solve problems like his dad did. But once his dad started yelling, conflict got worse. The same pattern was happening in Dave's marital relationship.

When Dave realized this was a learned pattern from watching his dad, he was able to make a change. Once his wife understood the origin of Dave's yelling, she was less upset. Dave wasn't a bad guy, rather misguided in his approach to problems. He didn't have a good role model when it came to dealing with stress.

The meaning behind certain actions can sometimes provide a needed understanding for the people in our lives. In my case with the Christmas tree, I knew my husband conceded to another year with a live tree because of the meaning the tree held for me. He was sensitive to my need and decided that it outweighed his need for less work. In Dave's case, the meaning of yelling helped him realize he needed new ways to cope with stress. Yelling didn't help anything and was ruining his relationship.

Before you get too excited, realize that not all conflict goes away if you share your backgrounds. But the sharing goes a long way in helping others understand you better. It is a starting point. At times, it might be enough.

Now, if you are thinking you have a lot of negative family baggage, don't worry. You can lose the family baggage. For example, people who grew up in homes of yellers like Dave don't have to continue that pattern. People who saw tempers rage can learn to stay calm. Learned patterns can be unlearned!

Just remember that families are a major influence on who we become and what we bring to relationships, but we are not victims of those patterns. Change is possible. To change, we identify the patterns and how they are used. Then we think about the meaning behind the pattern. Finally, we decide if those patterns are healthy and helpful to our relationship and talk about ways to do things differently.

Negotiating Conflict

Marriage is one place conflict is hard to avoid. The need for negotiation is great and can teach us a few general points about conflict negotiation—the need for love and respect. Ephesians 5:33 says, "However, each one of you also must love his wife as he loves himself, and the wife must respect her husband." Loving includes listening to and valuing the other person in a respectful way. Dr. Eggerichs, in his popular book *Love and Respect*, says that without love from her husband, a wife reacts with disrespect, and without respect from her, he reacts without love.[4]

Now take this principle into action. Men who love their wives listen to their opinions and accept their influence. In intimate relationships, listening and accepting influence is related to happily married couples. In fact, when a man accepts the influence of his female partner, the relationship goes better.[5] When a man doesn't accept his wife's influence, this is a predictor of divorce.

Why the man? Good question, because when a woman does not accept a man's influence, this is not a predictor of divorce. It may be that historically women have more readily accepted men's influence. Now we see a need for more equality in accepting influence in order for *both* spouses to be happy.

During conflict, the man's ability to yield some part of the conflict to his wife helps a couple work together and brings down defensiveness. Compromise is easier when both views are equally appreciated, but especially when she feels valued and appreciated.

So men, be willing to hear and do what your wife says. This doesn't mean husbands should agree with everything their wives say. It means that husbands should value and love their wives enough to listen to and consider their viewpoints.

On the other hand, I have seen a number of wives quick to point out how their husbands fail to meet their needs. They rarely compliment their husbands, don't ask for suggestions, and disrespect their intellect or attempts at repairing relationship problems. The fallout of disrespect is that it erodes love. Then when conflict comes into play, the wife is thinking, *He needs to change or this relationship won't get better.* The wife makes a disrespectful judgment: *If he would just do what I think is best, things would go better.* This is not mutual respect.

A helpful exercise is to list your core beliefs. Core beliefs involve the way you think about the world and people, including yourself. Once you identify your core beliefs, list what values you have related to those beliefs. Share those lists with another person and see how well they match with the core beliefs of that person. If there is a great deal of difference, talk through these differences.

To help identify core beliefs, follow your emotions. When you feel something strongly like fear of public speaking, follow that emotion of fear. What is it based on? Usually the fear is based on a thought that you will be humiliated, look foolish, or fall apart. Below that thought may be a belief, "I am not good enough." This negative core belief impacts your relationship because your behavior and thoughts will be based on those beliefs. When our core beliefs are negative, we become defensive and feel we have to defend ourselves. Defensiveness is a block to conflict resolution.

Here are examples of core beliefs in three areas. Use these to stimulate thoughts about yourself. Then write down your core beliefs and share them with an intimate other. Look for agreement and disagreement and if your beliefs are negative or positive. Positive beliefs with high agreement make conflict less likely.

BELIEFS ABOUT MYSELF

I don't deserve to be loved. I do deserve to be loved. Being loved has nothing to do with deserving.

It is unsafe to express my feelings. It is safe, and even encouraged, to express my feelings.

I am responsible for other people's feelings. I am responsible for only my feelings.

I am a loser. I am confident in Christ in me.

BELIEFS ABOUT OTHERS

It is important to please others. It is important to please only Christ.

People let me down and cannot be trusted. Most people can be trusted.

It's useless to try to change others. I can influence others toward change.

I will be rejected. I am accepted and unconditionally loved.

People are out to get me. People are kind and basically helpful.

BELIEFS ABOUT LIFE/THE WORLD

The future is hopeless. There is always hope in Christ.

The goodness of man will bring peace. Only God will ultimately bring peace.

I don't need to be concerned about the poor. Someone else will do what is necessary to help them. It is important to care for the poor.

What I do for myself is most important. What I do for Christ matters in eternity.

After death, there is no life. Death is the beginning of eternity.

Once you list your core beliefs, evaluate them in terms of Scripture. Do they line up with God's Word? If not, core beliefs can be changed. Read God's Word and immerse yourself in his truth. Believe what he says about you and to you. For example, the belief "I don't deserve to be loved" does not line up with God's Word. Scripture tells us God unconditionally loves us, not based on anything we do but simply because we are one of his children. His love has nothing to do with what we deserve.

Once our beliefs are more in line with God's truth, we will be more secure in who we are and how we see others and the world. This secure base makes us less defensive and more willing to work through conflict.

Handling Differences

When we disagree, we want the other person to affirm us, not fight with us. We want to be accepted, not invalidated. So when we become stubborn, fear we are giving up something, and don't accept influence, then the other person becomes the enemy and we begin to disengage emotionally. We mentally check out—a problem that can lead to estrangement.

When we stay with a conflict and work through our differences, we grow closer. This requires looking at our expectations, understanding our preferences, checking our assumptions, respecting differences, and talking about our beliefs and values. Then we can identify family patterns and decide if those patterns are good for conflict resolution or if we need new ways to think and behave.

5

Living Under the Cloud of Negativity

> I'm telling you. People come and go in this Forest, and they say, "It's only Eeyore, so it doesn't count."
>
> Eeyore, *The House at Pooh Corner*

Eeyore, the blue-gray donkey from the Winnie the Pooh tales, lives in the Hundred Acre Wood under an ever-growing cloud of negativity. He is constantly losing his tail and depends on his friends to help him find it. Even when people try to help, Eeyore finds a way to remain sullen, making him a challenging animal companion.

Do you know people who remind you of Eeyore? They are challenging to live with because of their negativity. No matter what others do, they look for ways to confirm their negative feelings.

Snappy, Not Happy

Dan and Karen fell into this negative trap. The first two years of marriage were filled with ups and downs, but they were hoping the arrival of their first child would stabilize their marriage. Most days, they ended up fighting about something. Neither could recall what they fought about, just that they went at each other on a regular basis.

Karen yelled and Dan checked out. Nothing ever got resolved because they couldn't find a way to be nice to each other when they disagreed. Both described their marriage as miserable, and wondered how in two years they arrived at this point. The added stress of the newborn sent them to my office.

Two years prior, I had counseled Dan and Karen during the first few weeks of their marriage. I saw the red flags and pointed them out. At the time, they thanked me for the feedback but decided they would give married life a try without addressing the negativity. This strategy of avoidance didn't work, and they were back in my office two years later.

"We're curious," Dan said. "What did you write down about us when you saw us a few years ago? We thought we were pretty happy back then. I know we picked on each other, but we never thought it would become a habit."

I pulled out my old notes and read what I jotted down. Karen began the fight by telling Dan he was a jerk. She was harsh and angry. Then Dan came back with a criticism of Karen. She defended herself, and both escalated the argument to the point of yelling. Physically, they looked like they were ready to explode. Neither one would calm down. Instead, they just stopped talking. Finally, Karen threw another verbal jab in an effort to engage Dan, but he refused. They turned away from each other, arms folded.

What I saw in that brief interaction was an escalation of intensity. This was a formula for trouble that was discovered years ago by marital researcher John Gottman and his colleagues at the University of Washington. With 91 percent accuracy, they could predict whether or not a couple would divorce after watching and listening to them for five minutes in a therapy room.[1]

I knew this research and recognized the problem. It wasn't that Dan and Karen were yelling. Happily married couples sometimes yell. It wasn't the fact that they didn't resolve the issue. Many conflicts never get resolved and people remain happily married.

It was the way they dealt with their differences that was problematic. First, they began the disagreement with harshness. It's hard to listen and stay calm when someone begins a conflict with a zinger or comes at you with guns ablaze. Most people immediately check out or become defensive. They feel attacked and want to fight back. This harshness doesn't help people stay calm and work through the issue. If Dan and Karen were going to make their relationship work, they had to approach conflict with a different start-up. It needed to be softer.

Second, they escalated their conflict from a mild state of irritation to an intense one—so intense they were physically upset. This is also a problem. Gottman and his group found that mild conflict that escalates is a relationship killer. In fact, he tracked this process in couples and named the progression the Four Horsemen of the Apocalypse.[2]

Criticism

The first Horseman is criticism. Criticism involves putting the other person down and implying that something is wrong with him or her. Criticism is different from a complaint. Complaints point out a behavior that needs fixing or addressing. A complaint is often a positive need, for example, "I need you to let me know if you will be late for dinner."

Criticism focuses on the person being the problem. It implies a deficit in character. For example, "You are completely insensitive to me when you come home late all the time." Just hearing this phrase probably would make most of us want to get away from that person!

Here is another example:

"Please, when you come home, would you help me with the kids? I'm trying to get dinner ready and need you to take them for a while. Is that asking too much?"

"It seems like the minute I walk in the door, I can't do enough.

I barely say hello and you are shouting demands at me. I know it's a crazy time of day, but could you at least give me a moment to breathe before jumping all over me?"

Sound familiar? When emotions run high, one of the most important things we can do is respond in a loving manner. One way to lower emotion is not to criticize. Resist that temptation to let loose, and stick with the facts.

"Honey, I need help with the kids when you come home. I feel overwhelmed and need you to take them out of my hair for about an hour."

Notice I left out, "Is that asking too much?"

Make your request and then assume the other person will be responsive. If they are not, then try to get their perspective before flying off the handle. Stay as neutral as possible and state your need. Keep defensiveness down. Maybe pause, breathe, and focus on staying calm. Once calm, try a little negotiation.

"I'm happy to help, but I need about ten minutes just to unwind, change clothes, and take a breath. Does that work for you? I promise I'll get to it and get the kids out of your way."

Notice that this response is not critical. Both people stay nice during the conflict. They are emotional, frustration is felt, but they keep that frustration from escalating and turning into criticism. They focus on their needs and try to present them in a way that doesn't cause defensiveness.

So next time a conflict arises, remember to stay away from criticism. Keep calm and present your request in terms of what you need. Have a little faith that the person might respond in a positive way and then negotiate. What works in marriage works in other relationships as well. Most people become defensive when criticized.

Defensiveness

When we criticize each other, we tear down the relationship and wear down trust. Negativity sets in. We may even negatively compare the person to someone who is kinder, gentler, or perceived to be more understanding. These negative comparisons in turn fuel the criticism. Thinking falls along the lines of, "*She never . . . He always . . . He's just like his father . . . She will never change.*" Defensiveness, the second of the Four Horsemen of the Apocalypse, is the result of such criticism.

It is a common reaction to respond with defensiveness when criticized. And when we become defensive, we don't listen. Blame goes back and forth like a ping-pong match. So much effort is spent defending our actions that there is little energy left to really listen to the issue. We defend by playing the innocent victim or attacking back.

Contempt

When criticism and defensiveness mark a relationship over time, we begin to feel contempt. We only focus on what is wrong with each other. We mock, feel superior, become sarcastic, name call, insult one another, and lose all respect. There is no appreciation for each other, only negativity. Of all the Four Horsemen, contempt is the one that does the most damage.

Contempt is so damaging to relationships that Jesus addresses it in Luke 18:9–14. He tells a parable to a group of people who felt self-righteous and despised people whom they considered less than themselves. In the parable, a Pharisee and a tax collector go to the temple to pray. The Pharisee, a religious leader, prays thanking God that he is not like others; he is not an adulterer, unjust, an extortionist, or even a tax collector. Tax collectors were thought of as thieves and despised by the people.

But in the story, the tax collector realizes that he is a sinner and in need of God's mercy and grace. He acknowledges his fallen state and asks for mercy. Jesus ends the story by saying that anyone who exalts himself will be humbled, and he who humbles himself will be exalted.

This principle rings true when dealing with differences. If you think you are better than another person, it is easy to feel contempt. It's the default mode of our hearts. Often we elevate ourselves as a way of ignoring our own responsibility for the problem. But contempt is void of humility. When contempt is part of a fight, it quickly shuts the door to unity.

Stonewalling

Eventually, when we criticize, defend, and feel contempt, we end up emotionally disengaging. Gottman calls this *stonewalling*, the fourth Horseman of the Apocalypse. We erect an emotional wall of stone, stop talking, and become distant. As a result, the other person may leave the argument. This distancing, whether physical and/or emotional, ends with unhappiness.

At this point, trust is eroded, disrespect has grown, and very little positive is even noticed in the relationship. Even neutral events are turned to negatives. Thoughts like, *The dishes need to be done,* turn into, *He expects me to wait on him and be his maid.*

When we live under this negative cloud, we feel hurt, frustrated, misunderstood, angry, disappointed, and victimized. We lose trust. Communication breaks down. Our relationship energy goes to defending ourselves, getting even, keeping score, and a host of other negative reactions. If something doesn't change, the relationship limps unhappily along or ends.

Dan and Karen were living under such a negative cloud. Sadly, they admitted they didn't trust each other anymore and had allowed themselves to be disrespectful to one another. They thought they were responding to the added stress of having a baby, but the negative interactions were not new, just intensified. The lack of sleep, physical exhaustion, and the 24/7 needs of the infant took a toll on an already negative relationship. In Dan's words, "We became snappy, not happy!"

Lifting the Cloud of Negativity

Once we recognize this cloud of negativity, it is time to turn things around. Begin by bringing up a problem without being harsh. For example, let's say you're upset because you got the car with an empty gas tank. Instead of beginning the argument with a criticism—"You never think about my time. Now I have to go to the gas station and fill up"—you could say, "I got the car with an empty gas tank and may not have time to fill it. Could you notice that next time and fill it when it's on empty?"

In the second example, you address the problem—the empty tank. You talk about how it will impact you and what your need is for the future. What is missing is criticism of the person. In any disagreement, "always" and "never" are *never* a good idea to use! This was the advice from my mother-in-law—lose those two words from any disagreement. They don't help. In fact, they typically escalate criticism.

Because beginning an argument with criticism or harshness creates defensiveness, concentrate on saying the complaint in a way that can be heard. A soft start-up will increase your chances of keeping defensiveness down. Here are a few examples of criticisms that begin with harsh start-ups.

> "We're going to be late because you are so self-absorbed. Think about someone else for a change."
>
> "You forgot to take your lunch to school. I can't depend on you for anything."
>
> "My boss called and you forgot to tell me? I'll probably get fired thanks to you!"

Now, rephrase these issues to soften the blow:

> "We're not going to make it in time for dinner if we don't get going. Could you please move faster?"

"You forgot to take your lunch? Okay, well, I forget things too. It's okay. Just buy lunch today."

"Did you forget to tell me my boss called? I'm worried about what he might have wanted."

When an argument doesn't begin with criticism, it doesn't automatically move to defensiveness. Defensiveness often includes that self-righteousness that characterized the Pharisee: "I would never be so self-centered," or "I don't take forever to get ready and make us both late." Self-righteous positions backfire.

We can also play the victim with statements like, "You never see my side of the problem," or "You are always right." This type of reaction does not help solve conflict. It only increases the tension.

To avoid becoming defensive, listen to the other person and decide if there is anything that the person is saying that possibly rings true. Could you have a part in the problem? Could there be some truth in what is being said? Owning your part decreases tension.

The antidote for contempt is reminding ourselves that we are no better than anyone else. It's staying humble. Humility is so highly valued by God that his own Son humbled himself and took the form of man to be in relationship with us. That humble act reconciled man to God. When we are humble, it changes the dynamic of a relationship and opens communication.

Humility requires us to acknowledge our part in problems—to confess to one another our faults and allow God's mercy and grace to fill our lives and relationships. Our lives can be transformed from self-righteous to humble.

When you lose the criticism, defenses go down, and feelings of contempt are avoided. As a result, that stone wall doesn't form. You are willing to approach the other person and not hide behind a wall for safety. And that is the point. The way you approach conflict keeps the walls down and the communication open.

Once the negativity of the Four Horsemen is eliminated or at least minimized, tension will ease. But this isn't enough to completely lift us out of the cloud of negativity. There is more work that must be done in relationships to deal with our differences, and this will be discussed in later chapters. For now, try to recognize criticism and minimize defensive statements and contemptuous zingers. Stay in the conflict rather than avoid it. Don't create distance by stonewalling.

Building the Positive

People who have constructive dialogues around differences do so because they keep the negatives down but also stay positive during a conflict. They come at each other with genuine respect, are willing to accept the influence of the other person, stay relatively calm or neutral, and remain connected.

All of this happens because two people have a friendship and genuine intimacy. During times of no conflict, they feel positive about their relationship. They can experience something negative but basically brush it off or try to be responsive to the complaint.

For example, if I feel negative toward my friend and he is late meeting me at a baseball game, I might think, *I wonder what he was doing. Probably something he wants to do because he rarely thinks about me.* But if my overall feeling toward my friend is positive, I might say, "No big deal. Hey, did something come up that made you late?" Notice, I don't assume some awful motive or behavior designed to irritate me. I give the benefit of the doubt and wait for a reasonable explanation.

A constructive dialogue can emerge from positive feelings, but a negative response will reinforce negative feelings. Seeing a person as your friend and not your enemy has benefits. It builds positive feelings. To be a friend, you have to spend time together and nurture your relationship.

Build Friendship

When couples are informally asked what would improve their relationships, the most common answer is that they need to spend more time together. In fact, couples who engage in *independent* leisure activities report poorer marriage satisfaction compared to those who do joint activities.[3] The same is true of most relationships. You have to spend time together to nurture the relationship.

So many people get lost in their day-to-day busyness and grow apart. Whether it is because of exhaustion, preoccupation, lack of interest, a time issue, or stress, losing touch is deadly to a relationship. Friendship is needed to deal with problems successfully. This is why people trying to improve their relationship satisfaction often find that spending time together does the trick. With couples, this is the thinking behind the Date Night movement—take your partner out on a date and have some fun.

Here are five suggestions that build friendship.

1. Ask the person about their thoughts, feelings, dreams, likes, dislikes, etc. How well do you really know this person? Are you tracking with his favorite movies? Do you know what her favorite flower is? Or are you too consumed with your own needs?

2. Tell the person what you appreciate about him or her. We often can get so focused on problems that we forget to say what we like and appreciate about a person. Praise reinforces the positive, so regularly tell the person what you admire, respect, or like about them.

3. Be emotionally available. Listen to what they are saying and be understanding. No one likes to be rejected or feel ignored. Friends care and listen to each other.

4. Do something novel together. Take a dance class, go for a walk on the beach, redo your very first date, have a picnic at the park, cook together, etc. Novelty brightens a dull relationship.

5. Share intimate details if you trust the person. Self-disclosure brings intimacy and pushes a relationship forward.

Praise Each Other Often

The power of praise is a principle most parents know when it comes to building esteem and healthy behavior in their children. Praise also builds positivity in our relationship with God. It focuses on what God has done for us and who he is. Since the qualities of God are only positive, acknowledging who he is builds our faith.

In Psalm 63, David is in the wilderness. Despite his negative circumstances, he says, "Because Your loving kindness is better than life, my lips shall praise You" (v. 3 NKJV). He chooses to praise even when life is tough because he knows that praise will refresh his heart and bring joy. Over and over in the Psalms, David chooses to praise and bless the Lord despite his negative circumstances.

Have you ever thought about the power of praise in your adult relationships? "Catch them being good" is an effective strategy to use with adults, not just your children. And yet, so many of us either focus on the negative or get comfortable with each other and drop off the praise.

Again, if we turn to the research of the Gottman Institute, we find how important praise is to sustaining relationships. Gottman and his colleagues found that in stable marriages there is a 5 to 1 ratio of positives to negatives. They call this the 5 to 1 rule—for every negative, there must be five positives to counter that negative. Then, when a conflict does arise, the positive is stronger than the negative and helps the couple stay positive.

In happy couples, the ratio of positive to negative is even higher—20 to 1. Happy couples are able to screen negative events because they focus on the positive and have a well of positivity from which to draw. Unhappy couples live under that cloud of negativity, with a ratio of .08 to 1 positive to negative.[4]

You may be thinking, well at least unhappy couples praise occasionally. True, but the power of the negative is so great that it takes more than one positive to counter the negative. It turns out that negative emotions stick around longer and have a bigger impact on us.

Now apply this to all of your relationships. University of North Carolina researcher Barbara Fredrickson confirms the importance of positivity. She studies how positive emotions can lead to a life of flourishing. She found that people who have a 3 to 1 ratio of positive to negative flourish. She talks about the importance of gratitude, love, playfulness, curiosity, and adventure, believing that these characteristics not only improve our relationships but also increase creativity and open us to new thinking and relationships.[5]

Dr. Fredrickson concludes that a steady diet of positivity changes relationships. The more positively we think and feel, the more we bounce back from adversity and even live longer.[6] The benefits are many. Looking at the glass half full is a good way to live.

To change a negative focus to positive, identify one area of your relationship that is impacted by negative thinking, for example, grooming habits, lateness, messiness, etc. Spend a few minutes every day thinking about the area you chose. Is there any part of that behavior you can spin positively? What are you saying in your head? Can you modify those thoughts? For example, *Yes, he misses curfew once in a while, but he also apologizes, calls, and has a reasonable excuse.* Then, think of what you could do to make the situation even more positive.

Someone I know does loving-kindness meditations. She thinks about the good qualities of people she knows. Actually, she is engaging in a biblical practice and doesn't know it. Philippians 4:8–9 says, "Finally, brothers and sisters, whatever is true, whatever is noble, whatever is right, whatever is pure, whatever is lovely, whatever is admirable—if anything is excellent or praiseworthy—think about such things. Whatever you have learned or received or heard from me, or seen in me—put it into practice. And the God of peace will be with you."

When the psalmist David felt under attack, he remembered to praise God. He meditated on God day and night. He developed a habit of gratitude and was mindful of God's presence. We can do the same and turn our negative thinking around. If God is with us and on our side, we have reason to stay positive. And when we choose to see others in a positive light, we end up happier.

In fact, University of Texas researchers found that when people wrote about their relationships for twenty minutes a day, for three days, they had a better chance of staying together. And when they expressed positive emotions in instant messages, they felt more positive.[7] These are simple steps with powerful results.

If you need to feel more positive toward another, try writing positive things. Then engage in a few acts of kindness like filling up the gas tank, making coffee, or picking up the dry cleaning. Boost the mood and build positive connections. A quick hug, a short back rub . . . do little things to make the relationship happier.

No one likes to live under the cloud of negativity. Not even Eeyore!

6

A Clash of Styles

Grow up. You're kingdom subjects. Now live like it. Live out your God-created identity. Live generously and graciously toward others, the way God lives toward you.

Matthew 5:48 (Message)

From the time we are born, we are in relationship. We depend on others to take care of us and meet our needs. The primary people responsible for caring for us are our parents. When our parents consistently meet our needs as children, a secure emotional bond develops. We aren't consciously aware of this bonding process, but it happens and affects our relationships throughout life.

We call this process emotional bonding or attachment. When these attachments are secure, they set the stage for trust, self-esteem, sharing, and support—all building blocks for healthy relationships. When we feel secure, we feel safe and know our needs will be met. The more secure we are in our early relationships, the more success we have emotionally bonding in our adult lives.

In terms of conflict, if we had parents who respectfully disagreed, showed affection, and acted in loving ways, we see our parents as people who can compromise and work through problems to the mutual benefit of each other. In our experience, differences are worked out and conflict ends well even if it isn't always resolved.

Feeling secure also helps us regulate negative emotions that rise up during conflict. When we feel secure, it is easier to acknowledge negative feelings and cope with them. Negative feelings can be tolerated and not seen as scary. We know that eventually those feelings will go away and conflict will get resolved. Consequently, secure people are more comfortable with the emotions that come with conflict and usually have developed constructive ways to resolve or handle them. Working through conflict is then seen as a positive thing.

Ashley and Nate felt secure in their attachments. So when tension mounted in their home over child care and responsibilities, both were able to sort through their feelings and talk about problems. Ashley felt Nate was not firm enough with the kids, making her the bad guy in parenting. Nate had a more relaxed attitude toward parenting, but he could see Ashley's point.

Both realized that their parenting styles clashed. However, they were able to calmly sit down and work through ways to be firm and relaxed, sharing the "bad" parent role. As they talked about this, there was no fighting, name-calling, or blame involved. The two realized their differences, talked about their parenting expectations, and compromised.

When people feel relatively secure in their relationships, they tackle conflict with confidence. But not everyone enters relationships with that confidence. Many feel a sense of insecurity that makes conflict more difficult to handle.

The Insecure Bond

When we don't feel safe and/or our parents do not meet our needs growing up, we develop insecure bonds. For example, if we grew up with a depressed parent who felt overwhelmed by life, our needs may have been neglected. As a result, we may not trust others to be emotionally available to us. We might be hesitant to talk about our needs because the possibility of no response is real to us.

Insecurity can also develop from a critical parent who focused on our weaknesses or failures or didn't feel we measured up to some unspoken standard. Insecurity can come from living with parents who are unstable due to addictions, abuse, or mental illness. It also can develop from inconsistency, lack of organization in a home, or neglect of our needs.

Feeling insecure affects our thinking and actions. It causes us to distrust others or worry about people rejecting or leaving us. We might become anxious when criticized, or even shut down when stressed. We might look to others for that missing nurturing or have difficulty expressing our feelings.

Insecurity can cause us to run away from difficulty and avoid others. When insecurity is in play, conflict can be seen as negative, anxiety-provoking, and something to be avoided. We might be reluctant to warm up to people enough to deal with conflict. Then we try to dismiss or deny negative emotions associated with conflict.

If you grew up in a family that was disconnected, meaning people did not have close emotional bonds, you might become aggressive and antagonistic when it comes to conflict.[1] Anxiety and insecurity can bring out hostility in some people. Conflict can be seen as a threat to independence, causing people to withdraw from others or downplay conflict.

To help us understand how we approach conflict, it helps to identify the type of bond (secure or insecure) we developed with our original families. Those attachment styles play a part in how we deal with conflict.

What Is Your Bonding Style?

As mentioned, people differ in their bonding styles based on their early experiences with caretakers and continuing experiences with others.

When we are young, we tend to idealize parents or caretakers. This tendency makes a child feel safe. But as we grow and enter adolescence, that idealization begins to break apart. We see our parents more realistically, with their strengths and their weaknesses. As we come to terms with the ways they let us down and built us up, we begin to find our own way and sort through the good and bad.

We realize that good parents promote communication that helps us grow. They are generally attuned to our needs and help us regulate and balance our emotional lives. This all works to form a secure attachment.

When parents or caretakers aren't able to help us balance our emotions or help when we feel down or hopeless, we feel alone, as if there is no one who can walk us through this important process of learning to regulate and balance our emotional lives. Then we become avoidant or anxious with conflict.

If you are a parent, maybe you are thinking that because of life circumstances and problems, you might have created an insecure bond with your child. The good news is it is never too late to make changes. Tune in to the child's emotional needs now. Be loving and responsive and you will create more security. If you have created a fearful environment in your home, create safety by working on issues that have led you to unintentionally hurt your child or make them fearful. You may be doing the best you can, but get help to make things better. You don't want to create feelings of harm, shame, or humiliation in your child because of your own problems. Your child needs a secure base from which to operate, so contact a local mental health therapist or parent training organization for help.

We all develop an insecure or secure bond in our families. And that attachment style is active when we deal with conflict. Two bonding styles make conflict difficult—anxious and avoidant. Anxious people worry that others don't love them and might leave or reject them. Avoidant people don't like to depend on others because people don't feel safe. We all live somewhere between these two extremes. The completely secure person is rare. We all have a little anxiousness or avoidance in us when it comes to relationships. To feel secure, you want to lower your anxiety and lower your avoidance.

People with high anxiety and low avoidance tend to be preoccupied and worry too much what others think. People with high anxiety and high avoidance tend to be more fearful. People with high avoidance and low anxiety can be dismissive and act as if they don't need others. So look at the markers below and think about your attachment style.[2]

1. Secure Type (Low Avoidance, Low Anxiety)

Secure people . . .

are generally happy in their relationships

are sensitive and responsive to others

think of connection as comfort and support

feel loved, accepted, and competent

can bring up issues and don't worry that their relationships are at stake

listen, value, and have empathy for other people

2. Preoccupied Type (Low Avoidance, High Anxiety)

Preoccupied people . . .

worry about what others think of them

don't consider their own thoughts and feelings

need to be close to others but do it in a clingy way

need validation and approval

are concerned that others don't value them

doubt their own worth in relationships

3. Dismissing-Avoidant Type (High Avoidance, Low Anxiety)

Dismissive and avoidant people . . .

deny their need to be close to others
need to feel independent and self-sufficient
minimize how important relationships are
hide their feelings from self and others
think of others in less than positive ways
cope by distancing

4. Fearful-Avoidant Type (High Avoidance, High Anxiety)

Fearful, avoidant people . . .

think of themselves as flawed, dependent, and helpless
think they are not worth loving or being cared about
don't trust others
expect to be hurt
want to be close to others but fear this
avoid intimacy
suppress feelings

Again, these are general descriptions. You may lean toward one style more than another. Now, let's take those general styles and apply them to a conflict situation.

Let's say that a teen tells his parents that he has to work late and will be home by midnight. It's 12:30 a.m. and the parents haven't heard from him. How would this play out with the different attachment styles?

The secure person would notice the time and think something made her teen late. The thought is, *He will show up any minute with a good explanation.*

The anxious or preoccupied person would wonder if she should call, maybe call someone else to check on him, or go out and find him to make sure he is okay.

The dismissive person wouldn't be all that concerned and go to bed.

At 12:30 a.m., the teen shows up. The secure person is happy to see him and waits for the explanation; the anxious person is a wreck by now and has imagined all the worst possible scenarios. She is mad and frustrated and starts accusing him of putting her through an ordeal. The dismissive person is upset that he woke her up.

Can you see why conflict is more likely with the anxious and dismissive styles? Communication is either nonexistent or accusatory. It focuses on what the other person is doing wrong (you woke me up, you upset me, etc.) or the anxiety of the moment. The thinking is "you better change in order for this not to be a problem."

What happens then is that the person who is being accused gets defensive. He may apologize just to get his parents off his back or try to be more secretive in the future to avoid accusations. Long-term, this doesn't work and ends in more conflict and distance.

A better strategy is for the anxious person to focus on her feelings and say something like, "I get scared when you come home late and don't call." This statement is more about how the teen's action impacted the relationship. Chances are the teen won't get defensive. When you talk about how the behavior affects you rather than blame, it is easier to move to solutions or keep talking about the issue. Defensiveness stays low, and this allows for problem-solving or nice talking. It also brings closeness and understanding.

Once you identify your primary way of relating, pay attention to your actions and words during conflict. Recognize the problem patterns like withholding your feelings, trying to avoid, expecting to be hurt, accusing, etc. Then you can work on changing to more positive reactions.

Finding Your Security in God

In terms of your attachment style, if you struggle with insecurity, don't despair. You can develop a more positive view of yourself that will then impact your relationships in a healthy way. The way you do that is to understand your identity in Christ. When you grasp what it means to be a child of God, insecurity begins to fade. So even if you did not grow up with a secure attachment, your relationship with God can heal that insecurity and anxiety.

God knows all your flaws and issues, yet still values you and thinks highly of you. He loves you unconditionally and accepts you through no action of your own. If you accept his love, it will change you. As your intimacy with God grows, you feel more secure. God's perfect love casts out fear and anxiety.

God chose you and loves you. He promises to supply all your needs and reminds you that, above all, you are secure in your faith (see John 10:28–30). You are constantly on God's mind (see Ps. 139:2), and he delights in you (see Ps. 37:4)! His promise is to never leave or abandon you. So live in the security of knowing you are one of his and that nothing can separate you from his love.

With his Spirit in you, you operate from his secure base. Other people may let you down, but God will not. He will never leave, reject, or abandon you, so there is no worry about any of that. He also wants to hear your cares and insists on taking your burdens from you.

Security in God also means your identity is found in him, not in what others do or say. No one but God has the power to define you. And he has already declared you righteous and one of his children. Our personal, living, and active God exchanges insecurities for his security. It's a hard deal to resist.

Furthermore, God in you makes it possible to act in ways that might not be in your range of experiences. For example, when you feel clingy and afraid to bring up an issue, God can give you the courage to confront and stay in the conflict. According to Scripture, he has not given you a spirit of fear, but of power, love, and a sound mind. You can confront anything with God's confidence. That is what David did when he faced the giant, Goliath.

First Samuel 17 is a familiar story. The Philistines are about to fight Saul's army (the Israelites). One warrior from each nation was selected to duel against the other. The loser's nation was to submit to the winner as their slaves. Israel's future was at stake—freedom or become slaves again.

Goliath called out the challenge. He was a scary man, a giant, nearly 10 feet tall, wearing 126 pounds of armor, carrying a spear as big as a fence rail. King Saul was the chief of the army and was expected to fight Goliath. But Saul was afraid and became depressed. He had no confidence that he could win this battle as he watched his army panic as well.

David, a shepherd boy, was tending sheep when he was given an assignment to take food to his brothers on the battlefield. David heard Goliath's challenge as he was delivering the food. He did what no other man would do. David accepted the challenge. He boldly asked who this uncircumcised Philistine was who defied the army of the living God.

His brother, Eliab, was surprised that David would be so bold. He called David a fool and dismissed him, but David didn't give in to the family pressure. His security was not based on his own abilities or war games or family validation. David was so confident that God is who he says he is that he told the people they would be delivered from this enemy.

Saul ran from the giant because he looked only to his own strength and came up lacking. He was insecure and fearful. David found his security in God and faced the conflict. The battle was the Lord's, and the enemy was defeated.

When you feel insecure, remember how God has helped you in the past. Remind yourself of his promises. Invite God into the battle. Put on your spiritual armor (see Ephesians 6) and don't run away. Be bold. The Lord, your God, is with you. The battle is his.

As you grow in God, your actions will be more characterized by the fruit of the Spirit—love, joy, peace, forbearance, kindness, goodness, faithfulness, gentleness, and self-control. Prayer and meditation help to keep you calm.

With a willingness to change and a heart open to God, you can lose that insecurity. Stop the patterns that don't work to bring closeness and conflicts to a peaceful place. Find people who are trustworthy; they do exist. And walk in the confidence that God is working things for your good.

Conflict Styles

While early influences play a role in your adult attachments, they don't determine the rest of your life. As you continue to grow and change, new experiences can change your attachment style. You can operate from a secure base.

Remember, conflict is shaped by our attachment styles. Our styles influence how we think, act, and feel and give us a way to understand why we react differently to different circumstances. Our feelings of security and insecurity are so important because they influence our conflict style. Marital researcher John Gottman says most people operate from one of three conflict styles—avoider, volatile, and validator.[3] Other styles include hostile, competitive, and accommodating styles. Let's take a brief look at these conflict styles. Even if you are not in a couple relationship, you still have a primary style that you bring to your relationships.

Avoider

Our first pair of people is determined to avoid conflict if at all possible. When I ask about problems, they look at me with a blank stare. They shrug their shoulders and tell me that eventually their problems have a way of working out. They don't talk about their differences much. They prefer to minimize and smooth over issues.

If they do bring up an issue, they present their sides, but then not much else happens. There is no attempt to persuade or convince the other. They are not angry at each other and agree that the positives of their relationship outweigh the negatives. They feel it is better to focus on the positives and prefer to avoid conflict as much as possible. When two people are both avoiders, this works for them.

Volatile

Our second pair is passionate, competitive, and intense. They love to argue. They are clear about their opinions and have no problem arguing and trying to persuade the other. Sometimes during conflict, they laugh, but then go back to disagreeing. They show both positive and negative emotions, but there is more warmth and positive feelings than negative ones.

They deal with differences head-on and see themselves as equals. At times they can be aggressive with each other. Their style is to be honest and to use conflict to better understand each other and strengthen their relationship. Even though their eruptions can be dramatic, they don't inflict emotional pain on each other and they lovingly reconcile. They are volatile but do well together because both are matched on conflict style.

Validator

Our third pair is calm and rational. They have conflict, bring it up, and work through it to a solution. They appear to really understand each other and make empathic statements that validate each other's opinions and emotions. They listen and show support and concern for each other. In the end, they compromise and feel like they understand each other better. They value each other and do well together because they both have the same style.

Hostile

There is one other style Gottman noted in his research. It is the hostile style in which conflict is handled with defensiveness, criticism, and contempt. People who use this style blame others and personally attack their character and behavior. This leads to a lack of connection and over time creates major problems in relationships—separation, divorce, loneliness, and unhappiness. This is not a style you want to adopt. A hostile style does not usually end well.

A Competitive Style

Maybe you are one who approaches conflict from a competitive win-lose style. Randy is like that. He wants to win an argument and doesn't think about how his need to win might affect the other person. This style isn't effective in terms of helping a relationship become more intimate.

A competitive style can easily become problematic when a person pulls out all the stops in order to win. Competitive tactics include lying, attacking, criticizing, denigrating, threatening, being sarcastic, and denying. Basically, a competitive approach is about doing whatever it takes to come out on top. This often comes at the expense of the other person. And remember, interpersonal conflict is not about winning. It is about understanding the other person and finding a way to work together. A little competition may stimulate two people to work on a problem, but the style itself isn't conducive to building safety and trust.

An Accommodating Style

Some people are naturally more agreeable than others. Renee is like this. She usually concedes during conflict if the other person makes a good argument. People who accommodate are able and willing to give up their own goals and ideas for the sake of working together. They make adjustments or give in. They also make good friends and companions.

However, if you are always accommodating, resentment can set in because your needs are not being considered. So while accommodation is a great relationship trait, it has to be balanced by your needs. Accommodation and compromise do help keep the peace but should be used only when you feel you can live with the solution. Otherwise, resentment may grow.

The Mismatch of Conflict Style

People differ in how emotions are expressed during conflict resolution. Some people are hidden and silent, others direct and expressive. People who have the same conflict styles seem to do better than those who are mismatched. However, the best style to adopt is a validating style. This style seems to work best in relationships.[4]

What is your primary conflict style? Do you avoid, validate, become volatile or hostile? Now think about the conflict styles of other people in your life. Do the styles match? What happens when there is a mismatch (a mixing of the different styles) of conflict style? For example, what if the avoider is married to a volatile person? Or what if a validator is in relationship with an avoider?

When a mismatch occurs, conflict can lead to a stalemate and ongoing problems. In order to work with different conflict styles, we all need to make accommodations. Here are guidelines to help with the different styles.

An Avoider with a Volatile Type. When an Avoider and a Volatile type are together, one tends to pursue and the other distances. It is important for an Avoider to understand that emotions tell us how someone feels. The best way to deal with an emotion is to work through it and tolerate it, not avoid it. The Avoider just wants to get away from someone intense, but the Volatile perceives the avoider as unfeeling. In order to work together, the Avoider should try to talk more about problems, even when this feels uncomfortable. The Avoider must embrace the idea that it is important to bring up problems and try to deal with them. It is also important for the Volatile to calm things down and not overwhelm the Avoider, because the intensity of the Volatile can sometimes scare the Avoider. If you are the Volatile type, work on keeping your emotions in check. Practice calming methods like prayer, deep breathing, etc., to bring self-control. When you get in an emotional mode, take a ten-minute time-out and relax a little. This will help the Avoider stay with the conflict.

A Validator with a Volatile Type. The Validator is looking for the Volatile person to listen more. The Volatile person wants more passion in the dialogue, so Validators need to allow for some intensity. Emotion that is impassioned but controlled can be useful in making changes.

A Validator with an Avoider Type. When these two conflict styles meet, the Validator pursues the Avoider, and the Avoider distances because they become overwhelmed. The Validator can encourage the Avoider to verbalize what is wrong. Reassure them that nothing bad will happen by bringing up an issue. In fact, it will help the relationship. Validators should communicate the need to know what the Avoider feels and thinks.

As we talk more about how to deal with conflict, you can identify your primary conflict style and the styles of those with whom you interact. You can talk about the differences and decide what the two of you can do to accommodate each other if there are clashes. Keep in mind that both people must be willing to do a little give-and-take in order to work with each other's style.

7

>-<

Solvable and Unsolvable Problems

The quality of our lives depends not on whether or not we have conflicts, but on how we respond to them.

Tom Crum

When Don saw Gail flirting with his co-worker, he was upset. The incident took place at a holiday office party. Gail's side of the story was that she was being friendly and doing nothing wrong. Don's perception was completely different. He thought she was flirting and giving his co-worker a wrong message. Differences in perception brought this incident to a head.

A little background information gave this argument perspective. Don's ex-wife had cheated on him with a co-worker. Her repeated infidelity resulted in a divorce. Gail, on the other hand, battled shyness and was determined to talk to people at the office party. If she could approach a few of Don's co-workers, she would meet her personal goal of being more extroverted. Don didn't notice that she also talked to several of the women.

When we sat down and discussed the two perspectives, both understood where the other was coming from and decided to make a few changes related to each other's concerns. Gail wanted to be sensitive to Don's history but also wanted to approach people in order to combat her shyness. Don wanted to be less jealous but was triggered by seeing Gail with a male co-worker. If Gail would reassure him that she was only "practicing," he could handle her interactions. Gail felt this was a reasonable request.

The conflict was born out of two different perceptions and needs. Don wanted to feel safe in his relationship and not worry about his girlfriend cheating on him. Because of his past hurt, he looked to Gail to reassure him that she would be faithful. Gail wanted to practice being more outgoing and assertive. She hoped Don would support her efforts.

Both described the same behavior—Gail approaching and talking to Don's male co-workers. There was agreement on what triggered the conflict.

The *meaning* of the behavior was important. Both assigned different meaning to the same behavior. Only Gail could say what was truly in her heart. When she was given the chance to explain, Don heard a different story than what he assumed.

Gail knew Don's history and understood why he reacted the way he did. But he needed to check with her to see if his assumptions were true.

Don loved Gail and wanted to support her. He knew that her passivity was causing her problems on the job. It made sense that she would use a social occasion to practice being assertive and approaching people.

What worked here is that both were mindful of each other. Because of their fondness for each other, they were able to brainstorm solutions and follow through. A minor conflict stayed minor and didn't blow up to a major issue. This conflict was solved with a little understanding, listening, and checking assumptions.

Sometimes conflicts are solved this easily. You clear up the misperceptions. You don't assume but check with the other person. You accept another point of view and agree on a solution. Other times, it's more complicated.

Solvable Problems

Paul and Bruce began arguing about inviting friends to their house. They were former college roommates renting a house to save money. Paul liked to have people over to socialize. He grew up in a large family and thrived on the energy of people in the house. Bruce was more private and didn't enjoy these get-togethers as much as Paul. He preferred to spend his free time alone reenergizing. He was an only child and liked the solitude.

Both had different needs and preferences. What made this conflict solvable was the way they dealt with their differences.

Bruce: "I appreciate all the help you give when we get ready to have friends over, but I don't have a need to have people over so often. Right now, we have someone over every weekend. I would prefer if we limit company to two or three times a month. That way, I have some alone time. What are your thoughts about that?"

Paul: "I'm glad you told me what this was about because I thought maybe you didn't like my friends or didn't want to go to the trouble. Wow, I read that wrong. How about if we leave one weekend free, and then leave the others open for possible entertainment? Maybe even twice a month is enough. We could try it. You know I do like to have people over. It's just a lot of fun, but I don't want to do that if that feels too intrusive as a roommate."

Bruce's approach to this conflict kept the emotional intensity down for these reasons: First, Bruce began the conversation with a positive. He appreciated how much Paul helped him prepare for guests. He started in a soft, not harsh, way.

Second, he didn't criticize Paul or blame him for anything. There was no finger-pointing. Instead, he talked about his own need and why he felt the way he did. This opened the door to understanding and kept Paul from becoming defensive. Bruce didn't think Paul was a jerk for having different needs than he had—his needs were just different.

Third, Bruce did a great job of describing the problem in specific terms—having people over every weekend. This is a concrete description of the problem, not a criticism. He stated the issue by defining it and saying how often it happens. He gave the facts.

Fourth, Bruce offered a solution—limit the frequency of company. This left room for negotiation. He also tied the solution to his concern for Paul's needs, a positive. Now, it was up to Paul to offer a compromise or solution as well.

Paul also began with a positive. Then he made a great relationship point—he can't read his friend's mind. When he tries, he can easily get it wrong. He started to assume but realized assumptions get him in trouble because they are not always accurate. So he appreciated that Bruce explained himself.

Second, Paul owned his part of the problem but asked Bruce what he thought. He solicited his input. Paul listened without getting defensive. Then he engaged in empathy. He knew his friend doesn't need to be around people as much as he does, so he put himself in his shoes. Maybe having people around every weekend was a bit much—this was what Bruce was telling him.

Third, he accepted the influence of his friend. Bruce was telling him what would help their friendship (respecting needs), and he accepted this as important. He didn't think, *Well he needs to get over this*, or *What is wrong with him?* or *He needs to think of me too!* He definitely did not think, *I'm right and he's wrong*.

Fourth, he offered a compromise. They could decrease company from four to three times a month, maybe two. He accommodated his friend's request because of his need. He can be with friends thus getting his need for socializing met as well. There is balance in this approach. Both needs are recognized, validated, and accepted.

During the conflict, Paul was humble, empathetic, accepting, validating, solution focused, and a good listener. Bruce started softly, described the problem in behavioral terms, expressed his need behind the conflict in "I" terms (not an accusatory "you"), validated Paul's need and accepted it for what it was, and offered a solution.

The two were able to compromise and work out the problem. And because Paul was so understanding of Bruce's need for space, Bruce offered to have people over three times a month. Paul's responsiveness impressed Bruce to push beyond his comfort level too.

Each person approached the other in a way that led to problem solving. There are several key factors in creating a healthy, problem-solving environment.

Identify the Need

Jenny felt like Justin's parents never accepted her as part of the family. Every now and then, they would make a mean dig at her. Resentment was building because Jenny didn't feel Justin defended her when this happened. He stayed silent when the put-downs came. When Jenny pointed this out, Justin accused her of being too sensitive. He didn't think it was a big deal.

Justin: "We don't live with my parents. Why do you let what they say bother you so much? Let it go. Just ignore them."

Jenny: "I can't ignore it. It hurts too much and I don't understand why they do that to me. I've only been nice to them."

Justin: "That's true."

Jenny: "When they do this, I need you to say something, not just sit in silence. Tell them that what they say is hurtful and take my side. I need you to support me, not tell me to get over it."

Justin: "I didn't know this bothered you so much. I didn't think it was a big deal. They've said insensitive things to me my whole life. I learned to ignore them."

Jenny: "I don't have a life of relationship with them. When they do this, it feels like they are unhappy with me. It bothers me."

Justin: "I know what you mean. I feel that way sometimes too. Okay, next time it happens, I'll say something."

Jenny: "I would appreciate that."

Justin: "And I'm sorry that I wasn't being more sensitive to how you felt."

Jenny: "I can't believe it doesn't bother you either."

Justin: "It does, but I try to ignore it because I don't think confronting it would do any good."

Jenny: "Have you tried?"

Justin: "A few times, but I backed off when my dad told me I was overreacting."

Jenny: "Well, maybe if we stand up together, it will make a difference."

This conflict was not so much about the in-laws as it was about a husband supporting his wife. If the couple focused only on what was the right thing to do, they could have gotten sidetracked and continued to argue. It was the meaning behind the conflict that was important.

When Jenny addressed the issue without accusations and criticism, Justin responded. Even though Justin started out defensively and tried to minimize Jenny's feelings, Jenny didn't take the bait and stuck with her position. She wasn't going to ignore the situation like Justin did. She pushed toward a solution to the ongoing problem.

Once Justin realized the hurt involved, he didn't try to talk her out of her feelings. Instead, he listened and responded to her request. However, had Justin stayed defensive, Jenny would have needed to stay on point. She could have said, "Justin, I am pointing out a problem here and please listen."

Either way, Jenny helped keep the conversation going. She kept the intensity down by being direct about what she needed rather than criticizing Justin's parents. She also did not criticize Justin.

Justin also made a relationship repair by telling Jenny he was sorry. Even though Justin wasn't convinced his parents would change, he agreed to support his wife. They stuck to the issue—Jenny's hurt and how to handle it. The couple was able to move the problem from an individual one (Jenny's problem) to a "we" problem. *We* have to be a couple and support each other. *We* have to have each other's back.

Conflict develops when needs are not getting met in a relationship. So try to identify the need. The need is usually related to feeling loved and accepted, being heard or wanting something specific in the relationship. Once you recognize the need, don't get sidetracked arguing about who is right or wrong or get distracted by some other issue. Instead, think of a way to meet the need.

Be Kind and Respectful

Problems are best handled when we talk about them respectfully. Disrespectful communication shuts down conversation. Emotions intensify and people escalate or withdraw. Things are said that are later regretted. When this happens, it helps to take a step back and regroup. When it comes to what you say during a conflict, think about how you would talk if this were your best friend, a boss, or a person in authority. Would you be more respectful? If so, change your words.

Here is an example: My friend brought her new puppy to my house one day. The rambunctious dog knocked over one of my favorite antique lamps and broke it. The lamp had sentimental value because it belonged to my mother. When this happened, I was very upset. However, because the person was my friend, I didn't yell, scream, or get nasty. I remained calm and respectful. I felt like lashing out, but I knew this would solve nothing and would hurt our friendship.

Yet we don't always give this same consideration to our intimate others. We might say, "I can't believe you did that. Why weren't you watching the dog? What's wrong with you? My lamp is ruined, and it's your fault. Thanks for being so careless!"

When you are tempted to lash out at someone you know or love, think before you speak. Control your tongue. Show respect. Respect increases the chances of resolving an issue and preserves the relationship. Allow for mistakes, knowing people aren't perfect, and conflict won't escalate.

In the Bible, James 3 talks about the advantages of bridling the tongue. The tongue is powerful and can bring life or death to a conflict. Words are important and can help or hinder a conversation. Choose your words wisely.

Repair the Relationship

In healthy relationships, people try to solve conflict and repair any damage to the relationship that might happen along the way. In the example of Justin and Jenny, Justin said he was sorry for not being more sensitive to his wife's need. That was a relationship repair. He did something to de-escalate the conflict. Relationship repairs are important because they say the relationship is more important than winning an argument.

Stepping away from a conflict until you can calm down and get a better perspective is another type of relationship repair. When one person is overwhelmed by the conflict, their heart rate increases, adrenaline flows, and blood pressure rises. When this happens, the person can't think, much less problem solve. So a brief time-out to calm down is a good idea. It prevents you from reacting to the moment in a way you may not want to—escalating to anger or withdrawing. Stepping away lowers the tension and gives you a chance to soothe yourself before continuing.

Repairs are also made when you acknowledge your part of a problem. Take ownership of your emotions, thoughts, and actions. When my friend's dog broke my lamp, she immediately said, "I should have had my dog on her leash when I came into your house. She is pretty wild. I am so sorry."

My friend owned her part of the problem. She offered a repair. My part was to accept the apology and stay calm. A broken lamp wasn't worth being nasty to a friend. Because we both did our parts, the friendship remained intact. The conflict did not damage our relationship nor escalate to an argument.

What about times when conflict does create ill feelings? How do you make repair then? The other person may not offer to make a repair. What if, for example, my friend offered no apology? When this happens, pay attention to how you feel. Then tell the person how you feel, but do it in a way that doesn't blame. For example, "That lamp meant something important to me," rather than, "I can't believe what you just did!"

Now, here is the difficult part. Even when you respond in a good way, you have no control over what the other person will do or say. You can only control your part. Sometimes that person will ignore and hurt you. When that happens, you either let it go or set a boundary. "I would prefer you not bring your dog to my house off a leash so this doesn't happen again." This is called *setting a boundary.*

Boundaries set conditions on a relationship. They are based on lines you feel cannot be crossed. When you determine your personal boundaries in a relationship, make them known in order to be treated with respect. If, for example, I didn't set a boundary with my friend and her dog, every time she visited I might feel resentment about the way the dog is tearing through my house. Setting a boundary is a way to say I don't like this and it needs to stop; please have some respect for my things so they don't get broken. Boundaries are very important when it comes to being mistreated by others. You can't stop a person from being abusive, insensitive, or rude, but you can say it won't happen around you by setting a boundary.

Maintain Self-Control

Earlier I mentioned being mindful of the other person. To be mindful means to stay present in the moment. When we stay present, we focus on the issue at hand and not on problems from the past.

When we are mindful, we are more aware of our emotions and what we are doing with them. We might feel aroused and get angry, but we can regulate our emotions and calm ourselves down. We can also attend to our thoughts and make sure we aren't allowing negativity to take over. We can stay nice!

Beth and Barb co-lead a women's group in their church. Each woman is strong willed and highly opinionated. They often clash in terms of the direction of the group. Beth was mindful of the way she reacted to the friction between them. Every week, when she noticed her anger starting to intensify during their planning meeting, she practiced deep breathing and distracting her attention to something positive. She knew that if she wanted to successfully discuss problems, she had to control her temper.

Her co-leader, Barb, used prayer to regulate her feelings. When she felt discouraged or defeated in the relationship, she prayed and asked God to give her grace.

Then, when Beth and Barb were in the middle of an argument, they could control their emotions rather than automatically react.

Beth made a big change from belittling Barb during arguments. She realized that when she did this, it created a lose-lose situation and wasn't godly behavior. Barb would stop listening because her words were wounding. She had to break this negative cycle for things to get better. She had to change her behavior.

Barb reacted to Beth's snide remarks by withdrawing from her. She did not want to stay in the conflict because she felt unsafe. In order to create a win-win in the relationship, Barb had to change her behavior too. She had to find the courage to set a boundary with Beth. Beth could not talk to Barb in a belittling way and expect her not to withdraw. She wanted to work through issues, but the terms had to change.

Self-control is a fruit of the Spirit and a product of one's faith relationship with God. It is a gift that comes from love. It is the ability to regulate our personal life so as not to be driven by pride or pleasure. When we have self-control, we do not allow attitudes, thoughts, desires, or bad habits to dictate our lives. Instead, our impulses are controlled by God's Spirit living in us. He gives us the power to overcome our natural impulses toward revenge and hurting others.

First Peter 3:8–12 tells us to be harmonious, sympathetic, affectionate, compassionate, and humble. Meditate on this passage a moment:

> Finally, all of you, be like-minded, be sympathetic, love one another, be compassionate and humble. Do not repay evil with evil or insult with insult. On the contrary, repay evil with blessing, because to this you were called so that you may inherit a blessing. For, "Whoever would love life and see good days must keep their tongue from evil and their lips from deceitful speech. They must turn from evil and do good; they must seek peace and pursue it. For the eyes of the Lord are on the righteous and his ears are attentive to their prayer, but the face of the Lord is against those who do evil."

Self-control, then, is a type of spiritual management. Because of God's Spirit in us, self-control is brought about through good judgment and sound thinking. It is a dynamic process that assists us in self-management of our emotions that direct us in our actions. A healthy relationship is one in which each person agrees to exercise personal discipline. This means doing the right thing when you don't feel like it, mastering your moods, and controlling your tongue.

At the root of many arguments is self-interest and self-centeredness, not love. But when we are motivated by love, we don't have to force our way or win our point. Love creates a heart of compassion and a willingness to work through difficulty and exercise self-control.

Stay Connected

The conflict between Robert and Cindy was more entrenched and more difficult to solve. Robert grew up in an emotionally stifling home. No one really talked about feelings, but the undercurrent of tension seemed ever present. Robert's dad was a critical and controlling man who ruled by fear. If Robert showed any emotion, his dad called him weak and proceeded to humiliate him. Consequently, Robert learned to shut down his emotional life.

One thing that attracted Robert to Cindy was her emotional expression. She was the opposite of Robert's father, warm and accepting of him and whatever he felt. She wanted to know what was going on inside of Robert. In the early years of their marriage, Cindy pushed Robert to talk about his feelings. Over the years, Cindy withdrew, feeling it was time for Robert to step up on his own.

When Cindy's elderly parents became unable to care for themselves, the burden of their care fell to Cindy. As the stress of seeing to their needs intensified, she needed Robert to be emotionally present. Instead, Robert shut down even more. Cindy was frustrated and knew she was becoming resentful. She didn't have the energy to push Robert to meet her emotional needs. Now, when she needed him, he wasn't emotionally available. More resentment grew.

Years passed and Cindy's mom died. Cindy was an emotional mess, and Robert sat silent. The distance between them felt like a gulf, so they came to therapy. Robert was emotionally shut down and Cindy didn't care. They were at an impasse and considered divorcing.

Solving this conflict was not easy. The patterns of distancing had been practiced over the years, and the couple had grown apart. But there was a distinct path to the disconnection, thus there was also a way back. This impasse resulted from two different conflict styles. When stress intensified, one person shut down, the other looked for connection. Once Cindy stopped pursuing Robert for that connection, he withdrew even more. He reverted to his old pattern of turning inward, not toward his wife.

Robert's lack of emotional expression was learned, meaning it could be unlearned. He didn't like feeling so isolated and relied on Cindy's emotional coaching. He knew he needed to try to connect with her during times of stress and was willing to try. He had to push himself to do this without her coaching.

Cindy had to decide if she would give this relationship another chance. Exhausted by family stress, she wasn't sure she was up for the challenge. Emotionally, she had checked out. Robert had become one more source of stress and not somebody she could turn to for emotional support.

Both had to make a move toward each other instead of turning away. They decided to take this step.

To do so, they had to create positive moments in their relationship apart from the stress and conflict. Both admitted that the relationship was so unfulfilling that they stopped trying and drifted apart. Now they had to find ways to grow together. So they started attending church again, went for walks, and played games at night. Gradually, they rebuilt connection. They talked about their history together and remembered the good times, looked at photos, and laughed. When it came time to talk about problems, they were ready and felt more positive toward each other. They had something to build on now.

Cindy confessed her resentment (a relationship repair). Robert asked her to forgive his shutting down and shutting her out of his life (a relationship repair). Both chose to forgive and move forward. Robert initiated conversations with his wife, regularly asking how she felt and what he could do to help her. He wanted to help but didn't know how. I encouraged him to begin by staying in the moment and listening. This wasn't easy for Robert. It made him feel anxious, like he didn't know what to do. But I worked with him to better tolerate the anxiety. Over time, he would feel more comfortable.

Cindy assured him that he didn't have to fix anything. She just wanted a listening ear and someone safe to talk to about the stress she was under. She also wanted Robert to share his struggles and triumphs. When he was silent, she felt alone.

The impasse broke. The couple worked together instead of turning away from each other. When it came to handling outside stress, they were now a team who helped each other. If they could turn toward each other when stressed, they could face problems together and not feel alone. Both wanted this type of connection.

Unsolvable Problems

Some relationship problems never seem to resolve. Typically these problems are about what we think we require in a relationship in order for it to work. These requirements have to do with our personality and beliefs. For example, we may think we need someone who is wealthy in order to be happy. Or perhaps we feel strongly that the person must share our religion. If these requirements are missing, we don't feel fulfilled and become unhappy.

When the desired requirements are missing, conflict can become deadlocked. If one person, for example, holds to the religion requirement and the other refuses to participate in religion, the two are at a standstill. They fight about the same issue over and over. Yet some people stay together despite the gridlock. The reason has to do with the way they talk about these never-ending problems.

Other times, there is some level of accommodation or negotiation that takes place in order to stay together. Maybe the person who wants a wealthy partner finds a way to make wealth on their own and stops expecting the partner to provide the wealth. Maybe the two who share different religions agree to respect each other and go to separate religious ceremonies. Maybe the "right" position shifts to a livable position.

Relationships with unsolvable problems do survive. People remain married or stay friends and agree to disagree. Unsolvable conflict is not a relationship killer unless it is handled poorly. Usually this means keeping your humor about the problem and not allowing negativity to rule the discussion. It also helps to understand the other person's point of view even when you don't agree with it. Most of us like to feel accepted even when there is disagreement. And certainly, your willingness to accommodate or tolerate differences goes a long way.

Problems "In Irons"

Years ago, I took sailing lessons on Lake Michigan. During the lessons, we found out what happens when you are out in the water and you suddenly come to a standstill. When the sailboat stops moving, we call this standstill being "in irons." The sailboat has no wind to move it because it is positioned directly into the wind.

The person at the rudder tries to move the boat by forcing it to the eye of the wind. The boat starts to tact but begins to fall off the wind again and goes back to "in irons." Movement stops and the pattern repeats. In order to create movement, the person at the rudder has to let go and allow the boat to sail forward enough to catch the wind again.

People in unsolvable arguments are like sailboats in irons. They are positioned in such a way as not to move. They have come to a standstill and use the same maneuvers that take them nowhere. Someone either has to let go or make a change for movement to occur. Two stubborn people who refuse to give in stay "in irons."

When conflict gets stuck, it's best not to force a change but to talk about the conflict in a way that doesn't destroy the relationship. If our dialogue is nasty and involves accusations, name-calling, criticism, contempt, and negativity, we may sail out of the gridlock but into troubled waters. But if we find a good way to dialogue respectfully about the issue, we see movement in a good direction.

Two maneuvers help: keeping a sense of humor and showing affection for each other. When both are present, conflict doesn't tear us apart and we don't come away from the conflict feeling disgusted or completely frustrated. We still like the person, even if we totally disagree.

Relationships involve accepting some differences and not making them constant points of contention. We don't have to solve every problem to have a healthy relationship. In fact, we have three options when it comes to problems that appear to have no obvious solutions. All three take us out of "in irons."

Our first option is to **change how we feel about the problem.** We may have to let go of anger or judgment and decide the issue isn't worth the damage it may create. For example, as much as Jason hated living with a messy wife, his wife was not changing. So Jason changed how he felt about the issue. It was no longer a problem that he would allow himself to get worked up over. Instead, he hired a cleaning lady once a month to make the house more livable. In the end, he decided this issue wasn't a requirement for the relationship.

The second option is to **accept the problem.** People with religious differences, for example, remain friends but agree to disagree over religion. The problem doesn't go away, but both parties tolerate differences. This was the case when it came to political arguments in my family. At some point, we agreed to disagree and stop beating each other up about our differing views. Our differences were not getting solved no matter how much we talked and tried to persuade each other.

The third option is to **be willful and stay miserable.** This solution means people live with the distress that comes over disagreement and ongoing conflict. Eventually, the irritation and aggravation of the issue escalate and the conflict doesn't end well. These are the people who divorce, separate, or leave relationships because they can't find a way to get along and coexist with their differences. They sail into troubled waters.

Getting Back into the Wind

When there is a commitment to solve a difficult problem, getting past the standstill takes some skill. After a fight, it is good to process what went right or wrong. Here is a checklist of twenty questions to review after a fight. Any of these areas can be worked on so you don't stay stuck in a negative pattern. Read through these and evaluate how well you did in your last conflict. Decide what to work on to make the conversation better the next time.

1. Did you begin the talk on a positive note?
2. Did you define the problem in descriptive terms and stick to the facts?
3. Did you ask questions to clarify the problem?
4. Did you keep the argument to one issue at a time?
5. Did you focus on the present and not bring up baggage from the past?
6. Did you identify your feelings or needs?
7. Did you validate the other person's experience rather than judging them as right or wrong?
8. Did you stay in the conflict?
9. Were you mindful of the other person?
10. Did you own your part?
11. Did you use "I" statements instead of "you"?
12. Did you express your emotions accurately, stating what you felt and why?
13. Were you empathetic?
14. Did you talk to the person with respect and kindness?
15. Did you treat the person like you would want to be treated?
16. Did you begin to offer solutions?

17. Were you willing to try to negotiate, looking at the pros and cons?

18. Did you stay calm or take a time-out to calm yourself down?

19. Were you able to tolerate distress and agree to disagree if necessary?

20. Do you still feel positive about the person after the conflict is over?

As you think through your last fight or conflict, look back and decide where you could make changes based on these questions. For example, can you think of ways to keep the intensity down and remain positive? Can you agree that solving a problem is less important than how you talk about it? Can you offer a solution and talk with respect?

Sometimes when solving a problem seems impossible, you can choose to drop the rope and end the tug-of-war. In tug-of-war, when one person drops the rope, the tension stops and the other person is left holding the rope.

Sue decided it was time to drop the rope with her mother. The tension between them was causing problems. Sue had confronted her mom many times on the controlling remarks she made about Sue's parenting choices. It did no good, yet Sue wanted a relationship with her mom. There were good times in their relationship, and her children loved their nana. So Sue decided to drop the rope. When her mom "advised" her on how to raise the kids, she simply answered, "Thanks, I'll keep that in mind." The tug-of-war stopped.

In some conflicts, the issue isn't worth sacrificing the relationship. Attempts to confront and negotiate change have failed. The relationship is in irons unless someone navigates out of the deadlock. Dropping the rope is moving the rudder. It keeps the relationship moving forward while you agree to disagree.

In 1 Corinthians 7, Paul addresses a major unsolvable problem of a believer living with an unbeliever. He calls us to peace and states that the way we handle the situation might bring a person back to God. Micah 6:8 tells us, "It's quite simple: Do what is fair and just to your neighbor, be compassionate and loyal in your love, And don't take yourself too seriously—take God seriously" (Message).

Sometimes the best solution is to drop the rope. Ask if it is important to be right or to show love. Mercy relaxes the tension of conflict. Forgiveness and patience ease confrontation. And love helps us to endure all things. Solvable or unsolvable . . .

> Love never gives up.
> Love cares more for others than for self.
> Love doesn't want what it doesn't have.
> Love doesn't strut,
> Doesn't have a swelled head.
> 1 Corinthians 13:4–7 (Message)

8

>◂

All in the Family

Feelings of worth can flourish only in an atmosphere where individual differences are appreciated, mistakes are tolerated, communication is open, and rules are flexible—the kind of atmosphere that is found in a nurturing family.

Virginia Satir

The Smiths bounded through the front door of their son's home and loudly proclaimed their arrival and excitement to spend time with their grandkids. Mark and Jane met them with smiles and mixed reactions. They loved it when Mark's parents visited, but there were always problems.

Mark's mom regularly told Jane how to parent the children. She was a confident woman who felt obligated to share her wisdom with Jane on everything from cooking to wardrobe decisions. Listening to her, you would think Jane had not been able to function as a mother until she arrived!

Mark's dad was an adventurer, armed with a host of activities for the family to do together. He scheduled the family time like an army drill sergeant. Up at dawn, out of the house . . . move, move, move! It was all very exhausting.

At the end of his parents' visits, Mark and Jane usually felt they needed a vacation. Mark was tired from running around all day, and Jane had to bite her tongue not to say anything she would later regret. Something had to give.

Mark's parents meant well. They loved the grandkids and made a point to visit often. The kids loved it when the grandparents came too, but Mark and Jane knew a conversation was needed. Yes, they wanted to spend time with their parents, but it felt like the family was being hijacked when they arrived!

Mark: "We have to talk to my parents. We can't do this every time they come."

Jane: "You mean *you* have to talk to your parents. I'm not saying anything. Your mother scares me."

Mark: "Scares you? Seriously? Don't let her steamroll you."

Jane: "Oh, and you don't do that with your dad? He's running you ragged and you don't put on the brakes. They're your parents. You talk to them."

Is Jane right? Should Mark be the one to bring up issues?

In-law relationships can be tricky and a source of ongoing conflict. We choose our spouses, not our in-laws. However, when you marry someone, you marry the family. In-laws are part of the package deal. In-laws can love or not love you; judge or not judge you; support or not support you, depending on how they feel about you and their willingness to adjust to a changing family picture.

Families have very different ways of doing things. Because of the differences, expectations usually have to be brought out in the open and negotiated. Expectations, as we have noted, can be a source of conflict.

Make Expectations Known

A couple marries, begins a family, and makes decisions about how they will establish their family. Consequently, they have to set boundaries with their original families. Their parents no longer run the show. This is the normal progression of leaving home and joining with another person.

What often fails to happen is making expectations known, on both sides. Families do what families always do and expect things to go like they always have. But the bringing together of two family systems means the couple is figuring out what to keep, discard, or form new from their original families.

In our story, Mark and Jane must decide how much they want their parents to dictate the terms of their visits. Do they want to let them run the show, put up with it all for a short period, and keep the peace? Or do they want to talk about expectations and negotiate a few things to make the visits more enjoyable?

Mark and Jane decided to talk about expectations. They had never done this and felt it was worth a try. They didn't want to feel relief every time their parents left. They believed they had a shot at making the visits go better for everyone. So why not try? Yes, they might rock the boat, but it would be worth it if *everyone* looked forward to their visits.

Before meeting with Mark's parents, Mark and Jane talked about what they considered a reasonable amount of activity during a visit—maybe one activity a day. Second, they discussed how Jane might respond to Mark's mom's constant advice. Jane decided she could handle some of the advice and would choose her issues. Her approach would be, "Mom, you have so much experience raising kids and obviously did a wonderful job raising Mark, but I would like a chance to do this on my own. Would you mind not telling me what to do so often? I don't feel like a good parent when you do that, and I'm sure that is not your intent."

Then the couple practiced. Mark pretended to be his mother and told Jane what to do. Jane rehearsed her response. Armed with a plan, the couple approached his parents as a team. Because it was Mark's parents, he took the lead. He began on a positive note, telling his parents how much it meant to them that they cared about the grandkids and spent time with them. In fact, he had a few ideas to make the visits more enjoyable. Mark asked his dad if Mark could make a suggestion. When his dad said, "Yes," Mark proceeded to ask if they could do fewer activities a day and spend more time relaxing in their home. One activity a day is about what he and the kids could handle. Would that be workable? Mark's dad agreed.

Next, Mark addressed the issue with Jane and his mom. "Mom, I know you want to have the best relationship with Jane, so I told her she could trust you enough to bring something up. Is that okay?" (Notice how Mark set the stage for his wife.)

Mark's mom responded with, "Of course." Jane proceeded, being respectful and kind in her approach but addressing the overbearing behavior. Her mother-in-law said she was a bit blindsided, not realizing she was being overbearing. She could see how her concern about the kids was undermining Jane's parenting and promised to do better. Jane told her how much she appreciated this and hoped they could always be honest with each other.

In this case, conflict was solved when Mark and Jane confronted their expectations in a positive and kind way. Now, I realize that most times, conflict discussions are not this easy or positive. However, defining expectations is a first step and sometimes solves the problem. As we learned, differences in expectations are one of the reasons people have conflict in the first place.

The push back you might get doing this comes when families don't agree with your expectations and/or refuse to compromise. Then the adult child needs to be firm, telling his parents that they might not agree, but they need to support him and his new family. The idea is to explain why you do what you do and hope they respect your way of operating your family. Not everyone will. This was the case with Nick and Dee.

Divided Loyalties

Dee and her mother-in-law did not see eye to eye on many issues. Nick's father had passed away, and his mother became bitter and angry. Her bitterness often came out toward other people. At times, she could be downright mean.

When Nick and Dee visited, the mother-in-law introduced Dee to a friend as her "fat daughter-in-law." Dee was horrified and didn't want to talk to her again. This put Nick in a tough position. He hated what his mom had done and knew it hurt his wife. He knew Dee did not deserve to be treated with such disrespect. But he couldn't turn his back on his mom when she was so clearly stuck in her grief.

Dee gave Nick an ultimatum. "Your mom can't treat me like this. Choose your mom or me. I won't talk to her unless she apologizes."

Most of us can understand Dee's position, but giving an ultimatum is not usually a good idea. In this case, Dee was forcing a choice that divided Nick's loyalties.

Nick tried to reason with Dee. "Normally, my mom wouldn't say something like this. I think you need to let it go and chalk it up to grieving." Dee replied, "Really, you're sticking up for your mom after the way she hurt me? Just because she's angry at God doesn't give her the right to talk to me like that." Dee had a point.

When in-law tension peaks to a hurtful spike, it often puts the adult child in the middle, forcing a choice in a no-win situation. Nick wanted to be a good son and a good husband.

In this case, I suggested Nick support his wife and the hurt she experienced. Let's say Nick was right—this was not normal for his mom, and the comment was related to her grief. That didn't excuse what she did, but it might help Dee understand more about her mother-in-law if she were open to understanding. Nick asked Dee to remember how his mother acted *before* his father died. Did she ever say mean things then?

Rather than cutting off the relationship, Nick wanted to try an intermediate step to resolve the problem. He would confront his mom and ask her to apologize to Dee. If he did this, would Dee be willing to forgive and try again? Dee said she would.

Nick and Dee also anticipated what to do if Nick's mom refused to apologize and continued to say hurtful things. Nick would set a boundary. His mom could not continue to treat his wife this way, even if she were hurting. She could get help if she needed to and do whatever it took to work through the grief. What she couldn't do was dump on his wife. Nick put the ball back in Mom's court. If she apologized, repair could be made.

Furthermore, unless Mom agreed to control her anger and get help, she couldn't talk to his wife or him. Nick offered a repair (the apology) and a solution (get help). Now, it was up to the mother to apologize. If she didn't, she risked alienating herself from her son.

Nick's intent was to honor his mom and help her through this difficult time, but not at the expense of using his wife as a punching bag. His first loyalty was to his wife. When he left his family and married Dee, she became his new family. And it was important for Nick to take the lead on this, because he had a much longer and intimate history with his mom.

Is it fair when someone treats you badly? No, but the right thing to do is to address it and try to work through it, not cut off the relationship. We don't repay evil with evil. We take the radical path of Christ's example. At the least, our approach to conflict must reflect our character, offering repair and choosing to forgive even when reconciliation is not offered.

Setting Those Boundaries

With difficult families, the best approach may be to set boundaries and keep out of harm's way. Judi had to do this with her alcoholic mother-in-law and former husband. Their actions were placing the family in harm's way.

Judi and Sean were married for ten years before Sean called it quits and left. The couple had three young children who saw their grandmother regularly on visitations with their dad. The problem was that Sean's mother was an alcoholic, and the two of them would drink during visitations, putting the children at risk. Both Sean and his mom refused to get help for their addictions.

When Sean brought the kids back from visits, Judi could smell alcohol on his breath. The kids told Judi that Grandma and Daddy watched TV and drank a lot of beer. Grandma would sometimes yell and tell them to leave the room.

Judi confronted Sean about his drinking, driving, and being inebriated while watching the kids. This put the children in danger and had to stop. Sean made excuses and stood up for his mother. So Judi had to set a boundary. She involved a social worker and a lawyer and refused to allow the children to visit unless both parties were sober. Supervised visits were ordered.

Sean's mom became angry. She called Judi names and told her that she was a bad mother for taking Grandma away from the kids. She lied to her friends and said Judi was bitter about the divorce. Like most active alcoholics, she externalized problems and took no responsibility for her drinking.

No matter, Judi would be respectful and watch her tongue. The temptation to blast her mother-in-law for her irresponsibility and for endangering her children was tempting. But she kept thinking about Romans 12 and knew she could not retaliate. Holding her tongue was a lesson in humility. Proverbs 18:21 says, "Death and life are in the power of the tongue" (KJV). She didn't want to bring more problems to an already difficult situation. Nor did she want to stoop to her mother-in-law's level.

In order to protect her children, Judi had to set a boundary and enforce it legally.

Preventing In-Laws from Becoming Out-Laws

In-law issues could fill the pages of this book. For years, I have helped people in therapy deal with their in-laws. During the writing of this book, I became a mother-in-law for the first time. Too often, in-laws are viewed as out-laws in families—I don't want that experience and I am sure you do not either.

Researcher Sylvia Mikucki-Enyart at the University of Wisconsin–Stevens Point polled mothers whose children were about to marry. She overwhelming found that moms were more worried when their sons married than their daughters.[1]

The reason for this was because moms felt more uncertainty and insecurity with the daughters-in-law-to-be, wondering how they might influence their sons when it comes to family relationships. Mothers also worried that the wife may change their sons in ways that would create distance. And daughters-in-law wondered about their mothers-in-law—are they talking about me, going to be too involved, etc.

When the two women dance around each other and don't work out their relationship, distance can occur. Sons and daughters need their mothers and new spouses to work out their relationships, because mothers-in-law can be strong advocates, helpers, and supports to a couple.

When it comes to in-law relationships, everything from unsolicited advice to serious mental illness can create conflict. Navigating your place in the family can be challenging at times. If you are fortunate to have great in-laws, pat yourself on the back. If not, here are a few tips to make those relationships work the best you can, keeping in mind that the only person you control is you.

Try to focus on the positive qualities of your in-laws. In Mark and Jane's story, Mark's dad brought a sense of adventure to the family. Mark's mom was very confident and assertive. Both had positive qualities that, if reined in, could be admired. Look for the positive traits in your in-laws and reinforce them in ways that are helpful to the relationship. This will build positivity and warm them up to you.

Be careful with your words. Do more listening than talking and ask questions about the family. The more you can learn about your in-laws, the more understanding you will have. Keep in mind that words are powerful and cannot be taken back once spoken.

When you're in the home of an in-law, don't assume what you can and cannot do or use. Always ask permission first. This shows respect and will prevent problems from erupting. Offer to help out; for example, do the dishes, clean up, run errands, etc., when visiting. Find ways to be involved and involve them when they visit you.

Appreciate your differences. Families approach life differently based on their beliefs, values, customs, and history. The more you learn about the family, the more you understand why they behave the way they do. Understanding is a first step in tolerance. So ask questions about their traditions, ways of doing things, and expectations. Recognize and respect differences unless they are abusive or damaging.

Use humor to break tension. If you can laugh at yourself and little things that happen, tension is less likely to build. I've seen this over and over in families that manage to get along. Laughter is good medicine. It boosts endorphins and keeps stress hormones at bay. Conflict triggers a stress reaction in the body, and humor diffuses it. It changes the mood, minimizes emotional tension, and reestablishes a positive tone.

Involve your spouse in talking through the conflict. Couples are in this together, so don't sit back and tell your spouse to simply handle it or ignore problems. Help him or her. Talk through strategies as to how to approach and solve problems quickly. But make sure those strategies are healthy. For example, a son should not ask his mom to avoid problems. Relationships don't grow that way.

Spend time together. As with any relationship, spending time together and working through issues strengthens bonds.

Don't bad-mouth the in-laws. As tempting as this might be, it doesn't go well when you are constantly negative about your spouse's parents. Your spouse will come to resent this, and it can also negatively impact their relationship with their parents. Remember, in-laws are responsible for creating the person you love. Don't put your partner in the position of having to divide loyalties, like Dee did to Nick.

Work on unsolved issues from the last visit and solve them before the next. Problem solve where and when you can. Have a plan. The more you can anticipate problems and plan ahead, the easier it will be. This will prevent resentment.

Don't give momentum to the idea that your in-laws don't like you. If you feel this might be true, address it. Begin by telling the in-laws you are trying your best and would like a relationship with them. Control your emotions, be respectful and honest, and prepare for a number of responses. They could apologize for treating you poorly, say they will work on the relationship, or even talk about issues that might be involved. They may also criticize, show contempt, or avoid. If this happens, there isn't much you can do. You tried and may not be able to have the relationship you would like. Then this becomes a loss that needs to be grieved. Maybe, in the future, they will soften.

Even with difficult, controlling, manipulative, emotionally and mentally unstable people, try to stay connected and be consistent in your character. You may have to limit your connection and establish boundaries for the relationship, but this is better than complete cutoff and requires you to continuously make efforts toward peace or connection. Yes, making an effort can be exhausting and may seem like it is futile at times. But if you want some connection, you may have to be the one making the effort.

It also helps to think about what might be going on from the in-laws' perspective. For example, your mother-in-law once occupied the role you now have. She raised her children and sent them out into the world. She does have experience, especially with your spouse. This doesn't mean she is always right, but she did do something right or you wouldn't have married her child. Treat her in a way that you would want to be treated.

Mothers-in-law know their relationships with their sons change when they marry whether they acknowledge this or not. They are no longer the exclusive woman in a son's life. They have to adjust to this change and open their hearts to the woman who now cares for their son. Not everyone negotiates this change well. Some fear they will lose their child or can't seem to let go. Others worry that all the years of pouring love into their child will somehow be lost with a new family. This is fear-driven. And fear triggers conflict.

To help, a son can reassure his mom that he still loves her and respects the role she and Dad played in making him the man he is today. The son can eliminate competition by clearly letting his mother know that his wife is now the most important woman in his life. However, Mom still occupies a special place in his heart and will always be his mother.

Sons and daughters-in-law do best when they are patient with the process of letting go and expanding the family system. To sons and daughters-in-law, I would say be careful and thoughtful as to how you respond to your in-laws. Hopefully, those relationships will last a lifetime.

Crossing the Divide

I regularly get letters and emails from mothers-in-law who tell me their daughters-in-law won't speak to them. They are heartbroken and feel helpless. Most times, they don't know what created the divide.

Refusing to talk to a family member because you are hurt or angry is immature. It's what kids do when they get upset on the playground. They try to hurt the person back. Grown-ups deal with problems. Consequently, when there is a breach in the relationship, the in-law should be told what caused the breach. This could lead to fixing the problem or clearing the air.

The reluctance to bring up the issue may be due to a lack of confidence that it can be fixed. I frequently hear this from daughters-in-law. They have little hope that the relationship will change, but yet they have not worked with a family therapist or tried to make repair more than once. A willingness to deal with the conflict instead of distancing is the first step no matter your gender.

Attitude is important. It takes courage to listen with an open mind and heart. If you approach conflict with the idea that this is probably a misunderstanding or misperception rather than some deep-seated character flaw, you will fare better. If the conflict *is* due to a deep-seated character flaw, the process will be more difficult and slower to repair. (See chapter 11 on dealing with difficult people.)

The longer the slight has been going on, the longer it will take to repair. Healing hurts takes more than a one-time conversation. Forgiveness and rebuilding of trust take time. Give it time and stay with the repair, especially if you have children. If you continuously reach roadblocks in the process, see a family therapist who knows how to bring reconciliation.

Honor Your Mother and Father

One of the Ten Commandments is to honor your mother and father (see Exod. 20:12). Honor is about esteeming another person. When it comes to in-laws or parents, we may not like them and/or find them difficult to honor. Even in the most difficult situations, we do need to find a way to keep this commandment. This doesn't mean always doing things their way, obeying all their requests, pretending not to have needs, permitting them to disrespect, control, or manipulate you for their own purposes. As mentioned, confrontation and boundaries are needed at times.

Parents usually do the best they can. Honor is not contingent on a perfect childhood or having parents who always got it right. Honor is about gratitude and respect for the difficulty of the job.

With in-laws and parents, you can honor them by pointing out the positives and reflecting on good times. An occasional call, a short visit, a card, or spending time together all help build positive relationships. And we know that the more positive the relationship, the better conflict goes. Extending grace, exercising forgiveness, and releasing judgments keep in-laws from becoming out-laws.

In the end, no one will congratulate you for taking the high road except God. He sees your obedience to his Word. Obedience isn't always easy. This is why Paul reminds us to not grow weary in doing good (see Gal. 6:9). In time, if we don't lose heart, we will reap the rewards of our good choices.

To those who feel like giving up on difficult family relationships, take a look at the example of the children of Israel. Even though God regularly showed up to rescue and provide for them, they complained and became disgruntled. This led them to wander in the wilderness and not enter the Promised Land. You may feel like you are wandering in a family wilderness and experiencing a desert in your relationships, but God is working.

Grumbling and complaining are signs of doubting God. Rarely do relationships proceed without some challenges. So when those challenges come, our response is to trust God to work them for our good and to be obedient to his way of responding. Our responses are what will be our responsibility.

When family treats you unfairly, focus on your reaction, the part you can control. What does God require of you? Can you do what Matthew 5:43–47 tells us to do? Can you grow up and live like kingdom subjects? These are challenging words.

I'm telling you to love your enemies. Let them bring out the best in you, not the worst. When someone gives you a hard time, respond with the energies of prayer, for then you are working out of your true selves, your God-created selves. This is what God does. He gives his best—the sun to warm and the rain to nourish—to everyone, regardless: the good and bad, the nice and nasty. If all you do is love the lovable, do you expect a bonus? Anybody can do that. If you simply say hello to those who greet you, do you expect a medal? Any run-of-the-mill sinner does that.

In a word, what I'm saying is, *Grow up*. You're kingdom subjects. Now live like it. Live out your God-created identity. Live generously and graciously toward others, the way God lives toward you. (Message)

Meditate on Romans 12:14–21:

Bless those who persecute you; bless and do not curse. Rejoice with those who rejoice, and weep with those who weep. Be of the same mind toward one another; do not be haughty in mind, but associate with the lowly. Do not be wise in your own estimation. Never pay back evil for evil to anyone. Respect what is right in the sight of all men. If possible, so far as it depends on you, be at peace with all men. Never take your own revenge, beloved, but leave room for the wrath of God, for it is written, "Vengeance is mine, I will repay," says the Lord. "But if your enemy is hungry, feed him, and if he is thirsty, give him a drink; for in so doing you will heap burning coals on his head." Do not be overcome by evil, but overcome evil with good (NKJV).

9

>◄

Parenting, Divorce, and Blended Families

To observe people in conflict is a necessary part of a child's education. It helps him to understand and accept his own occasional hostilities and to realize that differing opinions need not imply an absence of love.

Milton R. Sapirstein

Parenting

"He's thirteen. You can't talk to him like you did when he was seven."

"I know that, but he frustrates me and I find myself telling him what to do instead of listening first."

"But that doesn't work anymore, and the two of you just argue."

"Why can't he just do what I say?"

"He's growing up, developing his own thoughts, and testing the limits. This means we have to approach him differently."

"Great!"

129

Parenting seems easy until you have children. The emotions involved with the job often cloud what seems to be rational behavior. And just when you think you have a child development stage all figured out, the children grow into a new stage, requiring another adjustment in your parenting skills. This is challenging!

Now add another person into the picture. Both of you have to not only figure out how to parent your children but also be on the same page doing it. Yes, parenting is ripe for conflict.

Conflict between Parents

Parenting can bring on conflict between two parents who have very different styles and ideas about how to properly raise children. Parenting styles are learned from a person's upbringing and past experience. Different families parent differently. Some are more rigid than others, more permissive, more critical, etc.

When you marry or decide to have children, it is best to talk about the parenting styles you experienced and your ideas about raising children. Then discuss how you want to handle your current family. Are there ways of dealing with children you do not want to pass on? Ways of discipline you don't like or want to use? How do you each feel about spanking and punishment? How often should you praise and reinforce? Should you give consequences for the first offense of noncompliance or give a warning? These are just a few of the many questions to consider when becoming parents.

How you deal with the intensity of the conflict matters. Megan is only four but cries when her parents fight. She doesn't understand why there is so much tension, but she feels it. High conflict between parents hurts young children. When anger is evident between parents, for instance, preschoolers become physically, behaviorally, and emotionally upset. Their development is affected as the intensity of conflict impacts their attachments, beliefs, and their ability to process and regulate what is happening.

You can reduce negative effects on children if you make a few changes. First, physical aggression toward a spouse or child is scary in any family and especially frightening to young children. If you have a problem in this area, get professional help.

Second, children are upset when they hear awful things being said about a parent. So if they are in earshot of negative conversations, stop the negative talk. The best strategy is not to disparage a spouse in front of the children and keep children out of arguments. Certainly don't put them in a position to have to choose sides with a parent.

Some parents think giving each other the silent treatment is better than fighting, but children are aware of the silent treatment and are upset by it too. Children feel the chill and sense the distance. They know something is wrong and may think they somehow created the problem. So do not use the silent treatment as a strategy to deal with conflict.

The most important issue in parenting is creating unity. Unity involves agreeing on your strategies and enforcing them with consistency. Breakdowns occur when parents can't agree or are inconsistent. When you are in the middle of a conflict and tempers begin to rise, take a short break, talk through your strategies, and come to an agreement as to how to proceed. Say to the children, "Mommy and Daddy are going to talk about this and come back." This way, you present a unified front. It also models a problem-solving strategy for the children.

Parenting is an ongoing conversation. If you react without thinking and say something your partner doesn't agree with, you can always say, "I might have acted too quickly. Mom and Dad are going to talk this out and reconsider."

Furthermore, it is normal for kids to try to divide parents on issues. You will be challenged in the area of agreement. Even if you disagree in the moment, present a unified front and deal with the issue later. Evaluate whether or not the approach used was helpful and effective. As a couple, you may decide to change your approach. Do this together so you can both be on the same page and avoid the divide-and-conquer strategy commonly used by kids.

As children pass through development stages, the issues change and can trigger issues from your own childhood. For example, you may be overly reactive to normal teenage angst because of your behavior during the teen years. Maybe you were sneaky and now wonder if you are being duped by your teen. Yet, your teen may not be doing what you did or be secretive at all. Or let's say your father was heavy on the physical punishment. Any harshness by your spouse triggers you. When behavior triggers your past, identify those issues and separate them from the current situation.

Finally, if you can't come to agreement on how to parent as a couple, go to a family therapist for further help or enroll in a parent training class. I ran several parent training classes in which we worked on parenting skills and approaches. Parents reported that these classes were very helpful, like taking a driving class before getting on the road.

As you work through your parenting differences, remember you are modeling how to deal with conflict. If the model is negative and children do not see you work out problems, this is what they learn.

Conflict between Parent and Child

One of the specific issues we deal with in parenting classes is how different personality types influence parenting. In fact, your parenting style may clash with the personality style of your child. For example, if you are type A (driven and structured) and your child is more type B (relaxed and easygoing), this combination of personalities can be challenging. This is sometimes why a parent clicks better with one child over another.

Type A parents usually want their children to achieve and respond quickly to directions and consequences. Type B kids are more creative, laid-back, and tend to drag their heels on getting things done. Neither style is better than the other, but parents need to find ways to work with kids with opposite temperaments.

One way to accommodate both styles is to be creative and tailor your parenting style to the child. For example, a type B child does better when tasks are more of a game. Instead of ordering a child to empty the dishwasher, set a timer and play "beat the clock." The important thing, according to Reginald Richardson of the Family Institute at Northwestern University, is to balance high expectations with warmth and support.[1]

Parenting styles tend to fall in one of four categories: (1) Parents who are *authoritarian*. These parents have high expectations. Rules are expected to be followed. Authoritarian parents don't usually give children options and can lack warmth and nurturing. Their approach is, "Do it because I told you so." (2) *Authoritative* parents also expect children to follow rules but are much more responsive and democratic in the process. Discipline is supportive rather than punishing. (3) *Permissive* parents have few demands for their children and rarely discipline. These parents act more like the children's friend than their parent. (4) *Uninvolved* parents have few demands. They can also be rejecting or neglecting of children's needs.

Researchers have found that parents who are more *authoritative* in their parenting style have kids with fewer behavior problems, higher academic achievement, and less depression and anxiety. They tend to fare better overall.[2] This means the type A parent's push for order and getting things done should be balanced with fun, encouragement, and support. The driven type A parent has to be careful to show compassion along the way and understand that success can look different for different kids. The danger with pushing too hard is that children begin to feel that they aren't accepted for who they are and learn to conform to your dreams, not theirs. The best thing is to understand your child's temperament and help each reach his or her potential and passion, using a balance of pushing and accepting.

Sibling Conflict

Siblings are an important part of family life but are often over-looked when we talk about conflict. Yet siblings can help or hurt when it comes to learning how to get along with others. In fact, one study says that the more siblings you have, the better.

Sociologist Doug Downey at Ohio State University coauthored a study that looked at the number of siblings in a family and how that relates to divorce. What he found was that the more siblings you have, the less chance you have of divorce. In fact, each sibling lowered your chances by 2 percent. The thinking here is that having more siblings helps your social skills development. More siblings mean more practice negotiating conflict and working with other people.[3]

Now, before you decide to add more kids to the family, not all researchers are convinced that having lots of siblings is a preventative factor for divorce. The criticism is that one study doesn't constitute a definitive finding. Others feel that in today's age, children have many opportunities to practice their social skills away from the home. Thus, the playing field evens out, and sibling count isn't all that significant.

Whatever the case, if siblings help you get along better with people, the reverse could also be true. Siblings who fight and don't work out problems provide a negative model as well.

Sibling conflict is more of a problem than most parents realize. It can turn into a special kind of bullying that can have damaging effects if it isn't curtailed by parents. A study in the July 2013 *Journal of Pediatrics* found that kids victimized by their siblings are more at risk for depression, anxiety, and anger.

In the study, the researchers looked at four specific types of bullying: (1) mild physical assault, like being hit; (2) severe physical assault, like being beaten; (3) property aggression, like breaking a toy on purpose; and (4) psychological aggression, like name-calling. When a child was a victim of one or more of the above, they had lower scores on overall well-being.[4]

So parents, monitor your children when they interact and stop any repeated one-way bullying of a sibling. Not only will the sibling learn better ways to deal with his brother or sister, but you will improve the mental health of the victimized child. Your home is one place you have control over teaching children appropriate ways to behave interpersonally.

If more parents would discipline bullying in the home, we might see fewer bullies in school as well. This also means Mom and Dad need to model healthy relationships in order for children to learn conflict management.

To keep sibling conflict to a minimum and help them work through their differences, try these suggestions:

1. Hold each child responsible for their behavior. Don't let them justify being aggressive to a sibling. Set limits on what is right and wrong.

2. Referee arguments that get out of hand. Teach your kids to solve conflict without becoming aggressive. Let them work problems out without you, but step in when they cross the line.

3. Identify feelings of jealousy and envy, but teach your kids how to handle those feelings. Get at what is behind the feelings.

4. Reinforce the idea of family and taking care of each other. You have to model this on the parent level as well.

5. Fill your home with love and nurturing, praising often and tangibly showing love by spending time with your kids. A secure and safe environment goes a long way to preventing bullying.

Divorce

Jack Hayford, gifted pastor, teacher, and speaker, once posed the question: "Do marriage vows matter?" It's an important question that deserves our attention. Hayford believes that the church has swung from the pendulum of blackballing anyone who divorced to now having a less-than-concerned stance toward marriage vows.

This blur between secular and Christian views about long-term marriage begins in the mind and heart. When we entertain the lie that marriage cannot last a lifetime, we become disillusioned. Lies build on lies. Those lies work on our feelings and eventually alter our relationships. Over time, we "fall out of love."

In my experience as a licensed marriage and family therapist, most Christian divorces are not about abuse, repeated infidelity, or abandonment. Christians divorce over solvable problems. Christian couples say, "We've grown apart. We're not in love anymore." Divorce becomes the solution to unhappiness or lost passion. The Christian marriage, then, is not distinguished from the secular one.

Marriage is no longer seen as a covenant but a breakable contract. When the costs of marriage outweigh the rewards, divorce happens. The attitude is, "Time for a new partner who can better meet my needs and make me happy." Happiness is the ultimate end. Underlying the marriage vows is the unstated escape clause: "I'm outta here if it doesn't work out." In short, postmodern followers of Jesus have ditched the concept of a marriage covenant for the secular view of marriage as a contract.

The pull of cultural deception is like an undertow. Many fight this deception for a while but ultimately succumb to its strength. The problem with being deluded is that you rarely know when you are! If you believe marriage to be at best tenuous, divorce becomes a viable option. But if you believe the covenant to be sacred and honorable, then your marriage has a better chance at survival. Marriage will always have its unhappy times, but problems can be managed, forgiveness can abound, godly obedience can be manifest, and blessings can be restored when covenant is invoked.

I am not trying to put a guilt trip on anyone who has divorced. Rather my remarks are aimed at those who are contemplating divorce. I would encourage you to try to work through your problems utilizing every resource. Again, most problems are fixable when two people submit to God and have the desire to work through their differences.

In my book *I Married You, Not Your Family*, I identify ten popular cultural lies people use to support divorce. The first lie is that marriage is a contract. Most Christians say, "No, it's a covenant." But their behavior doesn't support their claim. Behavior follows belief. Too many react to marital difficulty by seeking an escape from their vows and refuse to see a marital therapist for help.

To think more about covenant, reread the chronicles of the Old Testament kings. The Israelites endured king after king. Good kings. Bad kings. Kings who behaved in despicable ways. But God in his mercy and grace maintained the covenant with his chosen people. His decision to do so was unconditional. Though he sometimes had to deal with his people's behavior through judgment, he never opted out of the covenant.

When we marry, we enter into a holy covenant before God with another person. Our mind-set should be "till death do us part" not "till I'm unhappy." Deal with the unhappiness but stay in the covenant. Without God, most marriages simply limp along. This is precisely why secular culture has reframed the institution of marriage to make it more disposable.

As Pastor Hayford reminds us, this mind-set leads to an onslaught of hellish delusions—more lies, more anguish, and more breakup.

It takes time to develop negative relationship patterns and time to undo them. The longer you wait, the more difficult it is. If you wait until you have emotionally checked out to see a therapist, marital therapy typically doesn't work. Yet, marital therapy is highly effective when couples go early and are ready to work.

If you are willing to go to counseling, find the right therapist who is trained specifically in couple's therapy. Some therapists who do marital therapy are not trained in it, so you need to ask about training and credentials. Look for someone who is a licensed marriage and family therapist (LMFT) to know that he or she is properly trained. This license means the therapist has completed the requirements of training to be a couple's therapist.

John and Ann had waited too long to go to therapy. When I asked them about the history of their relationship, they had nothing positive to say. In fact, all they remembered were problems. For years, conflict had spiraled out of control.

When John and Ann tried to talk about a problem, it didn't go well. Ann usually began with several statements of criticism. John became defensive and thought about how much he didn't like Ann. Ann would roll her eyes and believe that John was a jerk who didn't care. John wanted out of her sight.

The two were trapped in a negative cycle of criticism, contempt, and defensiveness. Overwhelmed with negative feelings toward each other, neither looked to the other for emotional care. Instead, they grew apart. Trying to deal with Ann upset John to the point that he felt the stress in his body. And Ann became convinced that someone else was better suited to meet her needs.

When couples get to this point, they usually call it quits.

John and Ann could be helped. These patterns are reversible. But they were unwilling to work on their relationship. To me, this is sad, because without the commitment to work it out, they simply became another statistic. Even sadder is that John and Ann have two young children who need their parents to work out their problems.

Children and Divorce

John and Ann's situation is a story that has been revisited many times in the postmodern American family. Who will get the children when divorce happens? In most cases, parents are able to work out the arrangements without major conflict. In other cases, conflict plays a major role. High conflict is a major risk factor for children in families of divorce.[5]

Tyler's behavior had begun to deteriorate lately. His divorced parents, Sam and Rhonda, were concerned about his behavior and sought help. The therapist told them that their unresolved conflict was causing Tyler problems. During the therapy sessions, the therapist pointed out how they have difficulty talking about their son without blaming and fighting each other. They couldn't parent because they were too busy demolishing one another's character.

Divorce didn't solve their conflicts, and Tyler was still caught in the cross fire of two people who hadn't learned to be civil to one another despite their differences. Tyler's behavior was a response to their constant fighting.

The first two years post-divorce are especially stressful and tumultuous. During this time, custody and visitation issues are front and center.

Custody Issues

Unfortunately, conflict is usually part of the story when it comes to deciding custody of children. Conflict can be productive when spouses put aside whatever negative feelings they have for each other and work out a plan that is in the best interest of the children. Destructive conflict usually involves threats, coercion, manipulation, and deceit, none of which help children adjust to a very difficult change.

When divorcing people feel misunderstood, maligned, or angered, they may not think clearly about what happens to their children because they are too busy defending themselves. In some cases, custody ends up looking like King Solomon's solution for the dilemma with the two moms who claimed maternity—threaten to cut the child in half and see who the real mom turns out to be. Unfortunately, some will choose to cut the baby in half rather than give in to the person whom they loathe. The real problem here is not the children. It is the unresolved anger of the parents.

A reader of one of my blogs sent in this question that gets to the heart of the issue: "My husband and I are divorced. We have a four-year-old daughter together, and I worry about how well my daughter is adjusting. My ex-husband is very involved as a dad and this is helping, but I still have so much anger toward him that I am not being very cooperative. I suspect this is a problem."

My answer: "You are absolutely right! Hanging on to unresolved anger toward an ex-spouse hurts you and your child. The importance of developing a cooperative co-parenting relationship with your ex-spouse cannot be overstated when it comes to helping children of divorce. Ask God to give you the grace you need to deal with your ex-spouse, to agree on parenting plans, and to reduce conflict. You may have to live out Luke 6—love your enemies, do good to those who hate you, bless those who curse you, and pray for those who spitefully use you. God will honor your response and give you sufficient grace."

When divorcing spouses continue to communicate, have a chance to work through problems, are not involved in marital violence or affairs, keep children out of the middle of conflicts, and try to make orderly decisions related to custody, the divorce process goes better.

In order to avoid persistent and bitter conflict, negotiation must be an ongoing process. Yet, negotiation was usually a problem during the marriage. Thus, to help the children, a mediator may need to be involved. Divorce mediators offer highly structured problem solving and negotiation. Mediators deal with differences and have good success. Studies show that three out of four couples headed for legal conflicts were successful at negotiating arrangements when they enlisted a mediator.[6]

Visitation Issues

Keep in mind that transitioning from one family to another is not an easy task for children. They may simply need time and space to adjust when they return to your home. It is not uncommon for children to feel anger, to withdraw or refuse to talk or eat, or even to throw a tantrum when they split their time between Mom and Dad. It is normal for the children to feel bad about leaving Dad or Mom's place to come back to their other home.

You should be supportive of the children spending time with their other parent. The children are adjusting to two homes now— one with Mom and one with Dad. So reassure the children that both parents love them and want to create a safe and secure home, and that both parents will remain involved in their lives.

You and your ex should talk about how the children are adjusting, reassure the children often, and help them process their feelings. Over time, children adjust.

Most important, stay in touch with what your children are experiencing and daily pray for wisdom. Keep God at the center of family life. He is your constant source of strength and healing. Be a family who prays and commits to working through even the toughest emotions and disappointments.

Parental Alienation Syndrome

In the 1980s, a forensic psychiatrist coined the term parental alienation syndrome (PAS) to describe the efforts of one parent to turn their children against the other parent. The syndrome involves deliberate mental and emotional abuse that can occur among highly conflicted couples who fight over custody. The result is a child who harbors tremendous negativity toward a parent that is not based on actual experience with that parent.

This is custody gone bad! Or a never-ending tug-of-war between parents that does not end well for kids. PAS destroys family bonds that once existed between children and a parent and is based on lies. There are no legitimate reasons why children are taught to harbor animosity toward the targeted parent.

It is a phenomenon familiar to divorce attorneys who listen to endless cycles of accusations and counteraccusations between spouses in child-custody disputes. A twelve-year study commissioned by the Section of Family Law of the American Bar Association of over 1,000 divorces found that parental alienation occurs regularly, 60 percent of the time, and sporadically another 20 percent.[7]

It usually takes the form of one parent blocking another from seeing the children due to a belief that children will be harmed by visitations. False allegations of child abuse and sexual abuse often are in play.

A less severe form of this is when a parent blocks a child from visitation due to the inconvenience of visits. Visitations are seen as a chore or an errand, not a means of promoting the parent-child bond. Over time, one parent is seen as superior over the other.

Accusations about the other parent are verbalized in front of the children, often describing that parent as dangerous or harmful or greatly exaggerating their faults. Examples of this are statements like, "I would give you music lessons, but your dad doesn't care enough to pay for them." Or, "Mom left because she doesn't care enough about our family." Children are sometimes told the other parent does not love them. Children then fall in line with this thinking and align with the parent who vilifies the other in order to preserve their relationship with the parent doing the vilifying.

Other times, alienation is due to false or untrue accusations of abuse against a parent who is blocked from seeing their children. False accusations can be severe, implying physical, sexual, or emotional abuse. Or one parent may frame differences of opinion as abuse. For example, a father may want his child to play soccer. The mother thinks this is a dangerous sport and calls the father abusive for wanting their son to play the sport. Or a parent may have different ideas about how late a child should stay up and one parent calls the other parent's decision abusive. No opportunity to accuse the other is missed. No benefit of the doubt is given. Such acrimony leads to alienating a child from a parent.

Another less obvious marker of this syndrome is when the relationship with one parent changes dramatically after a divorce. For example, if a dad had a positive relationship with his young children prior to the divorce, but it changes to a very negative one after the divorce and he has tried to maintain that positive relationship, something has happened to make that relationship change. Children do not lose interest in their parents or want them out of their lives unless someone is positioning that parent negatively (assuming there is not abusive behavior happening).

The motivation behind PAS is usually rooted in poor coping from the failed marriage. Instead of a spouse engaging in healthy grieving for the loss of the marriage, they engage the children in the ongoing battle. They feel so damaged from the breakup that enlisting the children in the anger and blame serves as a way to further the blame. Sometimes the spouse who vilifies feels so rejected and alone that they turn to the children for nurturing and support, even companionship. What emerges is a "we against the world" position.

Whatever the dynamics in play, the end result is poor conflict management and children who suffer the effects of parents who can't cooperate on their behalf. Children are left with fears, confusion, sadness, and despair because parents can't work through their disputes.

Custodial parents are charged by the law to avoid any disruptions with the children's other parent, yet, time and time again, we see this syndrome played out. If the target parent (the one being accused) avoids confrontation, the abuse isn't exposed and the alienating parent continues to abuse and set up further alienation. Grandparents, cousins, uncles, aunts, and other relatives of the target parent are all alienated and maligned to the children. Thus, the targeted parent needs to engage the courts in stopping this conflict and addressing the blockage that occurs.

If you see signs of alienation, continue to reach out to the children involved and don't give up on the fight. Your children are too important.

Helping the Children through Custody and Visitation Issues

Most divorced parents are concerned about the effects of divorce, separation, and remarriage on the development of their children. They already feel guilty about putting children through the ordeal of divorce and want to do whatever possible to help their kids adjust. If you are in this situation, a good place to begin is to reduce the conflict between you and your ex-spouse. I know you're thinking, *If I could do this, I wouldn't be divorced!* Possibly, but you still have to work on it for the sake of your kids.

The surprise for many couples is that divorce didn't make all those negative feelings go away. Negative feelings remain, making it difficult to make rational decisions concerning the children. It's no secret that parents unconsciously fight with each other through their kids despite knowing they shouldn't do this.

So how do you work on conflict reduction with an ex? First, try to resolve whatever unresolved feelings remain toward them. It's time to bury the multiple hatchets. Remind yourself that no matter how you feel about your ex, he or she is your children's parent. That fact doesn't change. Have positive exchanges around parenting issues. This will help build positive feelings in the children as well.

Always keep in mind that your efforts to work through conflict are pleasing God and helping your children. Your walk with the Lord is of utmost importance. If you hold on to old stuff, you'll create roadblocks in your intimate relationship with God and others.

To do this hard work, stay humble; putting your needs aside for the sake of your children requires sacrifice.

Also think about this: If your parents divorced, it is more likely that you will divorce. This is one of the biggest risk factors for divorce. Sometimes this is due to a lack of skills regarding conflict, dealing with emotions, compromising, etc. So if you didn't have great role models for interpersonal skills in marriage, go to seminars, be open to change, and learn to better communicate. This will help all your relationships.

In terms of custody, children can easily be drawn in to disputes between parents, lawyers, and extended family members. Thus, it is important to keep children out of what therapists call an unhealthy triangle. A triangle forms when two people have difficulty communicating or dealing with conflict directly and bring in a third person. The third person deflects the problem and becomes the focus of attention. The third person is often the child of warring parents. You break up unhealthy triangles by dealing directly with the person involved in the conflict.

Finally, divorced parents need to decide how much contact to have with each other. If negotiations can't be reached, parents who bring in the legal system are opening up an adversarial process that usually results in more conflict. This may be needed in high-conflict divorces, especially when violence, drug abuse, mental illness, etc., are involved, but do what you can to work things out apart from the legal system.

Blended Families

Terry slouched on my therapy couch and mumbled, "My mom has a new husband. She wants me to be nice to him, but I don't feel like being nice. I'm sick and tired of not seeing my dad. I don't like this strange guy walking around my house and telling me he's my friend. He's not my friend. He's a stranger. I want my dad back."

The challenge of living with a stepparent requires time and patience. Suddenly there is a stranger sharing the bathroom, giving directions, and checking your homework. Mom or Dad is no longer exclusively yours. Holidays become complicated. And what do you call this new person who shows up at the breakfast table with habits that annoy you?

From the child's point of view, their family has been torn apart and replaced with another. This loss and new arrangement were not by choice. Feelings of anger linger long after the parents' divorce is final. If the child hasn't openly worked through anger and unforgiveness toward the original parents, these feelings will carry over to the blended family.

Advice for Parents

The remarried couple is delighted to put their former marriages behind them and is hopeful about the future. Children of divorce are not in the same place. Often their feelings of rejection intensify when strangers enter the family. Remarried adults must constantly ask, "What are the needs of the children?"

While children need to be helped through the transition of blending a family, don't force closeness. The reality is that children lose a parent and parents gain a new partner. Talk about this fact. Encourage emotional expression. Reassure the children that no matter what they feel, you can handle it and will deal with their concerns. It takes time for a child to get to know a new adult and feel comfortable having him or her in the house. It's normal for a child to want the original family back so he or she doesn't have to divide loyalties, visitation, and important dates.

Blending families is no easy task, but we do know a few things that make the process easier. If you are in the process of blending or are already a blended family, consider the following.

Blending families is easier when there is a reasonable interval between marriages, allowing children and you to grieve the loss. People don't always give themselves enough time to grieve losses before moving on to new relationships. So don't be in a hurry to remarry.

An adjustment time of two to four years is normal. This may sound like forever, but it takes time for adjustments to stabilize. Generally speaking, the younger the children are, the easier it is to blend. Older children have a harder time adjusting to a new family.

Blending families is also easier if custody does not shift at the time of remarriage. If you can work out custody issues before the remarriage, it helps minimize the number of changes the children must undergo.

Children do best when they have contact with both their biological parents unless there is some major issue like addiction, abuse, mental illness, etc. Reassure your children that they will still see their biological father or mother. Because of the importance of contact, try to develop an open, working co-parenting relationship with your former spouse.

Blended families should not pretend to be a replacement family for children. For one thing, blending shifts a family's structure. For example, if a child's birth order changes in a remarriage, this should be addressed. Moving from the firstborn to a middle child in a blended family is a big deal because it changes a part of the child's identity and personality. An oldest, used to being in charge, may no longer be in command if they inherit older siblings.

One of the challenges of remarriage is that the old, intact, first family model is no longer a guide you can use. Remarried families are built around loss and must reorganize to a new family model. Plan for the complexity and ambiguity of roles, space, time, authority, membership—and the time it takes to negotiate these things.

It also helps to have both extended families approve the remarriage. The more buy-in from your extended families, the more support, encouragement, and help they will offer. If the families are not supportive, you have more obstacles to overcome.

Advice for Stepparents

As the new stepparent, you are an outsider to an already established parent-child relationship. You did not change the children's diapers or tuck them into bed every night, and you are not biologically related. Therefore you must be extra sensitive to appropriate physical boundaries.

Furthermore, you have had no time alone with your partner to develop what therapists call "middle ground," the area of agreement couples develop. You and your spouse must develop that middle ground by having many frank discussions about discipline and rules. Parenting must be authoritative, firm, and kind.

Discipline by stepparents can only occur after successful stepfamily integration. Early on, it is the stepparent's job to support the parenting choices of the biological parent. Usually the biological parent needs to be firm about their children following rules and being civil to you, especially in the early stages of marriage. You need to give input and monitor the children, reinforcing their biological parent's authority, but lending kindness and empathy to the children.

In the beginning, the stepparent's main job is to develop a relationship with the children. The insecurities and acting out of children may be a result of the disruption of the parent-child bond. Children have to share their dad or mom with you. This doesn't mean you relax or give in to inappropriate behavior. But it does mean that the biological parent should take a firm lead regarding what will be tolerated in your home. Over time, you will gain the children's confidence. Children will be able to understand what is expected of them in each household.

As we end this chapter, you can see that there are many family issues that involve conflict. It is my hope that you can find ways to lower the tension and work through issues. Most families operate with some level of dysfunction. There is no perfect family. But taking on family issues with a positive view of making things better helps keep family relationships intact and moving forward. Be encouraged to work on even the most difficult issues. Family relationships are too important to cut off or avoid.

10

Sex, Affection, and Conflict

> Good shepherd, tell this youth what 'tis to love.
>
> William Shakespeare, *As You Like It*

One of my favorite books is the classic *Wuthering Heights* written by Emily Brontë. It's a story of passionate love between Heathcliff and Catherine, who have known each other since childhood. When Heathcliff learns that Catherine has died, he feels deep anguish and cries out, "Be with me always. Take any form—drive me mad! Only do not leave me in this abyss, where I cannot find you! Oh God! It is unutterable! I cannot live without my life! I cannot live without my soul!"[1]

When I read this novel in my teens, I thought, *Yes, yes, I want someone to love me so passionately, he cannot live without me.* When I matured a bit, I read the classic again and thought, *Wow, there is some serious psychological disturbance going on in this romance!*

While novels and movies portray the undying, passionate love of characters like Heathcliff and Catherine, in real life, passionate love is intense but not sustained in such a way that our partners are roaming moors and calling out our names long after we die. Relationship passion ebbs and flows. When couples do not understand this and expect epic movie-like responses, frustration and disappointment end in conflict.

What I have noticed in recent years is that sometimes conflict can be avoided by having a better understanding of our gender differences in these areas. Men and women are wired differently when it comes to sex and affection, and those differences do matter. Knowing more about the differences of the sexes helps us be more empathetic and know what to do when conflicts erupt.

The Brain and Attraction

The brain is the center of attraction. It is also the command center for sexual attraction. This approximately three-pound organ is responsible for our enthusiasm in the bedroom or our waning desires and passions. Most scientists agree that healthy brain function is associated with more loving and sexual relationships. When parts of the brain are underactive or overactive, we can experience things like obsession, depression, and jealousy.

When we talk about sex and attraction, we are talking about a complex interplay of social, hormonal, physiological, psychological, and spiritual factors. All must be considered when we experience conflict in order to address the issue properly.

Helen Fisher, a biological anthropologist best known for her research on love, describes the sex drive as one of three different brain systems. The sex drive craves sexual gratification. The two other systems, romantic love and attachment, can be connected to the sex drive, but not always. This is why she says casual sex is not casual. Sexual union is more than a physical act. It also promotes feelings of love and attachment.[2] From a biblical perspective, sexual union creates oneness.

According to Fisher, romantic love is a drive, not just an emotion. When we fall in love, we exclusively focus all our energy and passion on one person. There is an intense desire to be with that person both emotionally and sexually. The intense feeling comes from the craving part of the brain and is more powerful than the sex drive itself.

This is why we are elated when a love relationship works, but equally upset when it does not go well. We pine away when rejected because that rejection is traumatic due to the intensity of emotions like sorrow. Think about it. People don't become suicidal over not having sex, but they do over romantic breakups. Furthermore, great poetry is written about romance and love, not sexual acts.[3]

Attraction

Mike knew he would marry Jordan the first night he saw her. She was working as a waitress at a local diner, putting herself through college. Mike stopped in the diner after a late night of work. He wanted some comfort food and knew the diner could serve up a good meat loaf. When Jordan came to his table to take his order, he couldn't take his eyes off of her. Something about her was so compelling. He claims he knew in an instant that she would be his wife one day.

Mike asked Jordan out, and as they say, the rest is history. She did become his wife, and two kids later, they are still in love and raising a family. At first, I was skeptical when Mike said it was love at first sight. But after reading more about the physiology of attraction, I see that this is possible.

Why we are attracted to one person over others is still a bit of a mystery, but here is what we know. In a room of waitresses, Jordan was the one who stood out to Mike. Something about her put him in overdrive and made him feel desperate to meet her and win her over.

Fisher says it takes only a second to decide whether you find someone physically attractive or not. We are drawn to those with similarities in intelligence, religion, economic status, and social values, and even to those who use similar words.[4] But love at first sight doesn't happen to everyone. It usually takes time to see if there's more to this attraction than the initial reaction.

At the beginning of a love relationship, love truly is blind. You see him across a crowded room and can't take your eyes off of him. The passion that burns inside helps you overlook the fact that he can't make a move without consulting his mother. Or maybe you think, yes, he has a bit of a temper, but who cares? I'm in love! And that initial desire burns intensely, rendering you oblivious to the red flags waving in the air.

Deep within your biology is a chemical concoction working to create this loving feeling. Your brain is being soaked by a "love cocktail," a powerful combination of neurotransmitters causing you to feel romantic love. Research psychiatrist Michael Liebowitz at New York State Psychiatric Institute provides specifics about this biochemical attraction. We meet someone to whom we are attracted. Our brains become saturated with a love cocktail composed of phenylethylamine (PEA—a naturally occurring neurotransmitter that acts like a natural form of speed), dopamine (a neurotransmitter that stimulates libido), and other excitatory neurotransmitters. This natural amphetamine state is triggered by infatuation or what many of us call romantic love.[5]

When we feel this attraction, this flooding of chemicals has the effect of euphoria. Our palms begin to sweat, our face turns red, our breathing becomes labored, etc. If you are thinking, wow, this sounds like what happens to me under stress, you are right. The chemical pathways are identical!

Love at First Sniff

Furthermore, smell can trigger arousal. Have you ever had this experience? You are at an event like a football game and get cold.

Your date takes off his jacket and wraps it around your shoulders, and you feel aroused. There is a biological reason for this.

There is a direct connection between the olfactory (smell) bulb in your brain and the arousal center of your brain. Smell stimulates the chemical called 4.16 androstadien-3-one (AND) that signals the brain for arousal. This chemical is found in men's sweat, hair, and skin and is why the scent of that jacket was arousing.

Your arousal in response to that jacket has to do with you wanting more diversity in your immune system genes.[6] In fact, a study by Claus Wedekind and his team found that women preferred the smell of a man whose MHC genes (a group of genes) were different from their own. In the study, he asked women to smell T-shirts men wore for a two-day period. The T-shirts were placed in a box, and the women were asked to sniff and describe the odors in terms of their intensity, pleasantness, and sexiness.

The women preferred the odor of men who had different MHC genotypes. In other words, they were more attracted to those men who were more dissimilar to them than alike. What one woman found sexy, another did not because of similarity/dissimilarity of the MHC genotypes. The idea here is that odor influences mate selection. Women choose diversity when it comes to genes, possibly as a way of adding genetic diversity to their children.[7]

Sustaining Passion

For years, researchers believed that the love cocktail wore off after about eighteen to thirty-six months, which would explain why romantic love burns hot in the beginning of a relationship and then simmers to the ember stage. This cooldown, if not understood, can leave a person feeling disillusioned and distressed. However, brain scans now reveal that romance can last beyond the effects of the love cocktail. In fact, we now believe long-term relationships can have that same passion as new love.

Sustaining passion, in part, has to do with bringing novelty into your relationship. When you do something new, you stimulate dopamine in the brain, and dopamine is one of those love cocktail neurotransmitters that brings feelings of romance. So while flowers and candy are nice favorites when it comes to romance, something new is the way to go. Go on a picnic, get massages together, take a drive to a favorite romantic spot, and create a memory that brings new passion to your relationship. Novelty will reignite love and prevent problems related to lost passion.

In addition, oxytocin and serotonin are two great chemical friends that help sustain your desire for a long-term relationship. They last longer than the excitatory chemicals and help relationships go the distance.

The good news is that you aren't at the mercy of your hormones. Your prefrontal cortex part of your brain, when healthy, gives you empathy and focus and helps you achieve the goal of sustaining a long-term relationship. When the prefrontal cortex is overactive, you can be obsessive, oppositional, and argumentative. When it is underactive, you can be impulsive, easily distracted, bored, and constantly looking for that attraction high. So take care of your brain, and your relationships will be better.

Dr. Daniel Amen, a clinical neuroscientist and psychiatrist, has a number of tips to keep your brain healthy and thus enhance your sex life. In his book *Sex on the Brain: 12 Lessons to Enhance Your Love Life*, he provides several tips to take care of your brain. A few examples include: treat any mental health disorders such as Attention Deficit Disorder or depression; think about what you are grateful for in your life and change your negative thinking; exercise and add a few supplements to your diet—for example, omega-3 fatty acids (fish oil) and l-tyrosine. To boost blood flow to the brain, try Asian ginseng, gingko biloba, and L-arginine and stay away from nicotine and caffeine, which decrease blood flow to your brain and genitals.

Desire

In some cases, desire differences are at the heart of conflict. One person may have much more of a desire for sex than the other. As a psychotherapist, I've treated numerous couples who complain of low sex drive or lack of passion in their relationships. Frustrated and even ashamed, they are bewildered as to how their once-passionate feelings for each other dwindled to almost nothing. The immediate assumption is that something must be terribly wrong in the relationship. There must be a deep, hidden emotional problem that only Freud could understand!

It's important for couples to keep in mind the role of testosterone. This steroid hormone produced by both sexes correlates strongly with desire. After the initial infatuation, when PEA (the love cocktail) wanes, testosterone levels play an important part in ongoing desire. Testosterone beefs up the area in the brain that is interested in sex, the hypothalamus. Women have lower amounts of testosterone than men and are more sensitive to the hormone. In women, testosterone is produced in the ovaries along with estrogen. Men have twenty times the testosterone levels as women, but their testosterone levels drop gradually with age.

Typically, men have stronger sexual desire than women. Of course, there are exceptions to this rule. More and more women come to therapy complaining that their husbands seem uninterested in sex, indicating that it is not always the man who wants more sex in the relationship. Low testosterone in men can decrease sexual desire.

An important difference to keep in mind is that men have a more constant sex drive that is heavily influenced by visual stimuli. In contrast, women's sex drive is more intense and stimulated by romantic words and fictional images.

Also, men usually need to feel physically close to their partners before feeling emotionally close. Generally speaking, women need to feel emotionally close in order to want to have sex. So you can imagine how this difference plays out. *Why isn't she more interested in sex? If she loved me, she would want to have sex. Why isn't he more interested in me outside the bedroom? If he loved me, he would help me with the kids, spend time with me, and talk to me.*

We'll discuss this more later. For now, in terms of the biological side of desire, remember this: Passion is short-lived; sexual desire is related to biochemical factors; and sustaining sexual interest is a complex phenomenon that includes your physical body as well as other relational factors.

What's Normal?

I laugh at the scene in the movie *Annie Hall* where the therapist asks the couple Alvy and Annie (played by Woody Allen and Diane Keaton) about how often they have sex. Alvy answers, "Hardly ever. Maybe three times a week." Annie answers, "Constantly. I'd say three times a week."

This funny moment highlights the differences between men and women and leads to the question most often asked: "What is normal? Twice a week, once a month, every day?" The answer depends on a number of factors, making a pat answer difficult. Things like medications, caretaking young children, lack of sleep, and more affect a person's sexual desire.

Conflicts arise when one person is unhappy with the quality, quantity, or both in his or her sex life. Expectations play a role, and when those expectations differ, letdown can creep into the bedroom. Then add stress, exhaustion, anger, resentment, pornography, and other factors, and a healthy sex life in marriage can take a hit.

The key for most couples isn't about having the same sex drive or being in sync with each other every time desire is felt. More important is negotiating the times when one initiates and the other refuses. It is during those times that each spouse should make an effort to meet the other's need.

Michele Weiner-Davis, in her book *The Sex-Starved Marriage*, says that a reluctant spouse can make a decision for desire. When couples prioritize their sex life and put energy into it by flirting, complimenting, and being nice to each other, things go better. In fact, many partners who are not in the mood get in the mood with a little prompting. The key, then, is to stay open and receptive.[8]

In terms of the question of frequency, forget the number and focus instead on how satisfied you are as a couple with your sex life. Dissatisfaction and disconnection lead to problems and should be discussed.

Sexual difficulties can be triggered by physical, emotional, or even stress problems. Thus, getting to the root of dissatisfaction is important. Things like busyness, boredom, childhood trauma, stress reactions, aging, and a host of other issues can lead to sexual difficulties and become points of contention.

Couples are often hesitant to bring up the subject of their sex life even when both may be dissatisfied. However, it is important to start talking, sleep in the same bed together, show physical affection to each other during nonsexual times, and make time for intimacy.

If you find yourself unable to make changes or even have a conversation about your sex life, consider getting professional help from a therapist who specializes in sex therapy. Doing nothing only continues the dissatisfaction and puts the marriage at risk.

Sex-Starved Marriage

Aaron and Holly were like many couples in the early years of child rearing. What was once a hot romance had fizzled to barely an ember. Before Holly became pregnant with their son, Hunter, she and Aaron had an affectionate and satisfying love life. Her attraction to Aaron was strong, and he enjoyed satisfying her. Aaron felt close to his wife and loved their time together. Often, their evenings would end with a sexual encounter that brought closure to the day.

All of that began to change when little Hunter was born. Taking care of an infant left Holly constantly tired, hormonal, and irritable. Her motherhood role felt all-consuming. Her mind was focused on meeting the demands of her new baby, not on Aaron's needs. Sex was the farthest thing from her mind. Exhausted, she would fall asleep early each night, leaving Aaron alone and feeling as if he lost his best friend.

As the weeks went by, the couple grew more and more out of touch with each other. Aaron even had moments of resenting his son. He knew those thoughts were irrational because he loved his son. Too embarrassed to admit to these feelings, he silently wondered if Holly was no longer attracted to him.

Eventually, the rejection got to him and Aaron gave up on making advances for sex. Holly felt lonely too and longed for the intimacy the couple once enjoyed sexually. Eventually, the couple decided to talk about the issue and agreed to therapy. They hadn't had sex for almost nine months. Both questioned whether or not they were still attracted to each other and wondered why their sex life had diminished to nothing.

This sexless marriage was not about lost attraction but more about the couple growing apart given the stress and changes they were experiencing. When I asked Holly if she was still attracted to Aaron, she said, "Of course. But I can hardly get a shower, much less think of sex." Aaron was relieved to hear this and explained how the loss of intimacy affected his feelings of closeness and connection.

When Holly heard more about Aaron's feelings, part of her was relieved. She felt the distance but didn't know how to revive their lost connection. Her husband was unhappy, she was consumed, and their sex life had suffered. Holly even wondered if her rejection of Aaron sexually was putting him at risk for an affair at the office. That thought was too scary to entertain but yet was in the back of her mind.

Holly told Aaron that she needed some prompting and time to get in the mood in order to switch her attention from the baby to him. He listened and responded. To her surprise, the more she opened herself to his advances, the more her own feelings of sexuality were reawakened. She too had missed the physical connection and noticed that when she was intimate with Aaron, he was more attentive to her needs.

Before therapy, Holly wondered if she suffered from a low sex drive. Now, she realized that her sex drive was still intact but took more planned attention to stimulate. This couple was not mismatched in their desire for sexual intimacy but had allowed the stress of the newborn to grow them apart. Both needed to adjust to the changes—and be more open and attending to their sex life.

The danger of withholding sex is that it births feelings of resentment that can accumulate over time. Couples who avoid each other by going to bed at separate times, blame and argue over sex, and make excuses for being uninterested are worsening the problem. I've heard couples say things like, "You no longer excite me" or "If you would be nicer, maybe I would be more interested." The danger in these types of remarks is that they only blame and do not resolve the issue. Blaming is criticism, and criticism is the first step on that road to emotional distance.

Finally, if you need motivation to get back into a healthy sex life, consider this: Sexual climax has an antidepressant effect. Yes, climax calms the same part of the brain that an antidepressant does. People who have regular sex tend to be less depressed![9]

Sex Is Not Always about the Sex

Helen Fisher discovered that people who fall in love view sex as secondary to other factors defining their relationship, unlike in unions driven by lust. In fact, 64 percent of individuals surveyed responded that they disagreed with the statement that sex was the most important part of their relationships.[10]

Intimacy involves both affection and sex. Sex therapists will tell you that a mismatch in sexual desire is the number one complaint they receive from couples. However, at the root of the complaint is often a mismatch of intimacy needs. For example, some people are fine with less openness, emotional support, sexual contact, or affectionate expression.[11] This is important to keep in mind, because when intimacy needs are matched or compatible, the couple is less likely to engage in conflict.[12] When intimacy needs are mismatched and are not met, tension and conflict build.

Those expectations usually relate to the *quality* of attachments developed in a person's life. Generally speaking, when a person has a secure attachment style, they are less likely to have problems than someone with an anxious or avoidant attachment style.[13]

Creating an environment of affection is important to the sexual health of a relationship. Affection has to do with how a person expresses love and fondness. It is a sign of caring. Both adults and children need affection to feel loved.

The way affection is shown may include hugs, kisses, flowers, cards, words, gestures like opening the car door or walking hand-in-hand, etc. Dr. Gary Chapman, in his popular book *The Five Love Languages*, talks about identifying your partner's primary love language in order to effectively express affection. The five primary languages include positive verbal reinforcements, spending quality time together, giving gifts, doing simple acts of service, and physical touch.

Dr. Chapman notes that one love language is not better than the other. Instead, love languages tell us the primary way a person feels loved and receives affection. Knowing what someone's love language is allows you to express affection in a meaningful way to that person.[14] For example, if a spouse is moved most by touch, then touching will be received as a way of showing affection. When touch is absent, the person may question being loved. Just as a note: Even if your love language is not primarily touch, physical touch of any kind raises the brain's oxytocin levels. Oxytocin is the hormone produced in the brain associated with maintaining healthy relationships, and it creates a feeling of contentment and promotes bonding and attachment important to sustaining a relationship.

Conflicts arise when you do not express affection in ways that have meaning to the other person. Thus, it is important to talk about your needs in this area—what type of expression do you like, and how often do you like it? Then commit to action.

For Men and Women Only

In my thirty years of clinical practice, I've heard two main complaints about sex: Women feel their husbands are only affectionate when they want sex, and men say they don't get enough sex. These complaints have to do with the way men and women think about sex. For men, sex is a way of showing affection. For women, affection comes before the sex.

Sex is a different need than affection. My friend Shaunti Feldhahn and her husband, Jeff, surveyed the differences between men and women in terms of affection and sex. In their books *For Women Only* and *For Men Only*, they summarize these differences based on nationally represented surveys, focus groups, and interviews with hundreds of men and women.[15]

According to their findings in *For Women Only*, men use sex not only to meet physical needs but also to meet emotional needs. This explains why in the middle of some emotional crisis, men think about having sex. For example, Aaron wanted sex when his wife was exhausted and stressed. It was not because Aaron was an insensitive, uncaring man. Rather, his way of wanting to connect with Holly again was to have sex. For men, lovemaking brings closeness and feelings of being loved, relieves day-to-day stress, and builds confidence. When the world is coming down on him, he thinks that if he has more sex, then things will go better—a stark contrast to the way women think.

Most women don't think of sex as a way to meet their emotional needs. Thus, they tend to think men are insensitive or uncaring when sex is pursued during an emotional time. The woman is thinking, *Hold me, sit with me, talk to me, and reassure me.* The man is thinking, *Let's get to it, and you'll feel better.*

Sex is so important to a man's emotional well-being that when it is withheld in a marital relationship because of problems, he can become withdrawn and depressed. His sense of feeling loved is at stake because his way of communicating with his wife is blocked. This can result in feeling lonely and inadequate.

Helen Fisher tells us that when sex is withheld, men do not have the chemical stimulants to give them that sense of well-being. Having sex and regular orgasms make them feel better due to the testosterone boost. Basically, sex assures a man that he is loved.[16]

In terms of desire, men want to feel desired by their wives. Initiating sex is one way a wife can say she desires her man. And when a man feels desired, his confidence grows along with a sense of well-being in other areas of his life. Sexual rejection or lack of response to a sexual move is often interpreted as rejection of him as a person.

According to *For Men Only*, women lead with their feelings, not their anatomy. A woman needs to feel attractive and desirable. Desirability is greatly helped by men expressing heartfelt compliments. Compliments and understanding a woman's inner life, her wishes, desires, intentions, etc., bring intimacy.

In Aaron's case, empathizing with the massive changes Holly was experiencing helped him understand her difficulty in transitioning from baby to him every night. Knowing that Aaron was attentive to her and understanding of the stress she was under helped Holly feel affection again.

Recently, I had a conversation with a young artist on this very topic. He didn't understand why his wife didn't want to have sex as a new mom. "She's rarely in the mood and complains about being tired all the time. Honestly, I don't see it." His cure for her stress? Have sex more often.

The more we talked, the more I realized that he genuinely believed that if she would make time for sex, she would be less stressed. This was his way of helping her reduce stress.

Men and women must realize that their sexual wiring is different. Because women have much less testosterone than men, they are not turned on simply by looking at a man, even when he is attractive. But just because women have lower sexual desire due to less testosterone doesn't mean they aren't attracted to their husbands. Like in the case of Aaron and Holly, the wife is usually receptive to having sex under the right conditions, but may not initiate. Remember, she isn't thinking, *Let's have sex to reestablish our closeness.*

So in terms of sex and affection, differences do abound and can lead to conflict if not understood or addressed directly. The bottom line: Don't give up on your sex life. Make it a priority. Get rid of distractions and make time to focus on each other. Both men and women need to feel validated and loved. They just go about getting their needs met differently.

Betrayal

Before we move on to another topic concerning conflict, we have to talk about betrayal. Betrayal is devastating and includes more than sexual cheating. It usually signals a problem related to loneliness and lack of validation. As difficult as it is to talk about, betrayal is a relationship problem that must be confronted and then, hopefully, repaired.

Affairs

Infidelity is typically the result of something that has been simmering below the surface of a relationship. For example, discontent, loneliness, and resentment are produced by negatively comparing the person to someone perceived to be better. Unfortunately, as this negativity builds, the people involved are not always aware of it.

Then someone comes along and shows interest, validates the person, maybe even admires the person. When the betrayer engages this person and turns away from his or her partner, the process of infidelity begins. Closeness is building with an outsider, and the negative comparisons get stronger. The partner's emotions are ignored, and distrust has set in. The negativity feeds the thought that maybe their spouse is not the right person for them. This other person understands them better. The person is now ripe for betrayal.

Secrets are kept. Conflict is avoided. Emotional distance grows. A coalition with another person is formed. Distrust marks the original relationship. The betrayer has to justify their actions and thoughts by continuing to turn away from their partner and blame them for unhappiness. A line is crossed.

Both men and women cheat, but men are more sex-focused in their cheating. However, most affairs are not about the sex but have more to do with feeling lonely in a marriage and turning to someone who validates you. This does not ever justify an affair or take responsibility away from the person who betrays, but realizing why helps couples understand what has happened in order to know how to repair.

Betrayal can be fueled by all sorts of relationship issues—marital dissatisfaction, family problems, friendships that have become too close, physical proximity, spiritual decline, convenience and sexual stimulation, need for love and validation, and more. Betrayal is more about friendship and emotional connection. It involves purposeful behavior that is rationalized and justified.

Helen Fisher's work on the brain systems related to love helps us understand that without God and a commitment to marriage, we can easily wander into tempting waters. She reminds us that our brain's systems of attraction, romantic love, and attachment aren't always connected to one another. Based on her research, she believes we are capable of loving more than one person at a time. In fact, she says we can lie in bed at night and swing from deep feelings of attachment for one person to deep feelings of romantic love for somebody else.[17] Thus, the decision to stay faithful has to include a vibrant spirituality in which we overcome temptation and the urge to turn away from our spouse through the power of the Holy Spirit.

When a sexual betrayal happens, it is devastating. The breach of trust is enormous, and we know that sex is never truly casual but instead creates a biological bonding with another person. The covenant relationship is broken. This makes the work of repair difficult but not impossible.

In my book *I Married You, Not Your Family: And Nine Other Relationship Myths That Will Ruin Your Marriage*, I outline the way back from a sexual betrayal if a couple is willing to make repair. I remind readers that divorce is never commanded in the Bible, but forgiveness is, and reconciliation is God's heart. Reconciliation cannot happen if forgiveness is missing. When couples are willing to repair the damage, it begins with admission of the affair. This is not an easy step. People react with anxiety, anger, grief-like symptoms, and more. The reality of an affair awakens a deep sense of loss for the betrayed spouse.

It is important to allow the betrayed person to feel whatever comes and to work through those feelings over time. The intensity of the feelings will eventually diminish. Prayer helps. God knows your pain and is a source of comfort. He can bring peace to your mind when your thoughts are centered on him.

The betrayer needs to be prepared to share remorse often and allow questions. They must give needed reassurance whenever requested and be empathetic to the pain caused through their actions. Patience is needed as the couple works through the root of the issue. The betrayed person needs time to process and question.

After the admission of an affair, the betrayer needs to make sure that every aspect of the affair has been stopped. I call this the "no more contact rule." If a spouse can't agree to this, it indicates a lack of remorse or ambivalence regarding reconciliation.

Next, acknowledge the feelings related to the crisis and, as painful as it is, tell the story in whatever level of depth the betrayed person wants. Then identify what made you vulnerable to this wrong action and work on rebuilding after forgiveness.

If you are the one who was betrayed, then part of that rebuilding means letting go of judgment. Too often, a partner forgives but continues to judge the person. Let God do that! Go back to the basics of working on friendship and building positivity in the relationship. Don't ignore what happened, but once it has been dealt with, don't use it as a club over the person's head.

Forgiveness is an individual act, but reconciliation requires a mutual restoration of trust. Can the relationship be put back together? With God's help, it can; I have witnessed this many times. In Joel 2:25, God promises to restore the years the locusts have eaten. God can do miraculous things in the lives of people who repent and desire reconciliation.

Pornography

The other day I pulled a weed that was growing into my front porch. It looked harmless, so I reached for it and yanked it out. Unfortunately, the weed turned out to be poison ivy. The rash spread all over my arms and face. After a number of days, I looked a little like the Elephant Man because of how severe the rash became. I itched and was in pain. Finally, I called the doctor for a steroid to help with the swelling.

There was a moment when I looked at the poison ivy and thought, *This might be poisonous* (leaves of three, let it be!), but in my impulsivity and lack of judgment, I threw caution to the wind and touched it. It took only seconds of contact to create the pain and suffering but weeks for the rash to go away.

Some things that appear to be harmless have a toxic touch. Dabbling in pornography or a flirtatious relationship falls into this category. Both may seem harmless when you first look or engage but end in serious negative consequences.

Scripture tells us to flee from temptation. Do we do this? Do we turn off that movie that is causing us to lust? Do we stop the advances of our office mate, knowing we are playing with fire? Do we go to a party and drink too much and later regret our actions? Temptation is like the beautiful ivy plant. It looks healthy and harmless but is toxic when touched.

The apostle Paul exhorts us, "Let not sin therefore reign in your mortal bodies, to make you obey their passions" (Rom. 6:12 KJV). When our passions become slaves to the wrong things like pornography, they become selfish idolatry. Pornography enslaves people and ruins relationships.

When we talk about pornography and its impact on relationships, there is nothing healthy or positive that can be said about it despite efforts to present it as harmless. The effects of pornography on marriage are well documented as being destructive and negative. My advice is not to start with it or buy the lie that a little pornography can help a marriage.

I disagree with some of my secular counterparts who advise couples that a little porn can rev up a relationship. I can't support objectifying another person as a healthy way to enhance mutual pleasure or desire. Pornography undermines the respect of a person. It detaches a person from his or her body, reducing the person to an object or commodity. Neuroscience proves this.

Researchers Susan Fiske and Minka Cikara from Princeton and Jennifer Eberhardt from Stanford did MRIs on a number of male students in order to image their brains when they looked at various photographs of women. The part of the brain that activated when the men saw bikini-clad women was the part associated with objects or "things you manipulate with your hands." Pornography reinforces "women as objects."[18]

Pornography stimulates the brain like an addiction. You get a hit and then need more to give you that sense of pleasure. The need for more arousal grows as people tend to move from viewing to doing. The craving invades their thinking and can lead to lost interest in sex with their spouse. The hiding and turning toward another person or object for arousal hurts intimacy. To add insult to injury, the biology of desire leads to emotional connections with the images or people involved in pornography.

Researchers at Emory University studied the brain when pornography was shown to men and women. They found that the amygdala (the part of the brain that is involved in controlling emotions and motivation) was much more activated in men than women when sexual material was viewed for thirty minutes. However, both sexes reported similar levels of interest.[19] This explains why men are more captivated by porn. This doesn't make men victims of the visual images, because they can override those images by using another part of the brain to divert their attention. But it does explain why more men are hooked on porn than women.

If you need another reason to stay away from pornography, researchers found that flooding yourself with pornography stimulates the drive for casual sex. Men who use porn are more likely to have multiple sex partners and extramarital sex. This is based on a theory called "sexual script theory." The theory proposes that watching porn defines your view and expectations of "normal" sex. Viewing porn is like a rehearsal for how to get pleasure with a script provided.[20]

Masturbation

I know we have a difficult time talking about masturbation, yet it is a source of conflict for couples as well. The problem with masturbation is the sexual fantasy that goes along with it.

The Bible is silent on the topic of masturbation, but in Matthew 5:27–28 Jesus speaks to lustful fantasies. He tells us that to look at another woman with lust in your heart is adultery.

So the question is what do you think about when you masturbate? Some men tell me that they only think about their wives. When I ask if those thoughts are about past experiences or fantasies about what she might do, if they answer the latter, I tell them that this may set up unrealistic expectations that can create conflict in the area of sex.

Here are the major problems concerning masturbation: (1) It involves lustful fantasy that is self-centered and is not about satisfying mutual desires in a relationship. (2) Masturbation involves sexual thinking that stimulates parts of the brain that can develop a tolerance. Our bodies adjust to that tolerance, and we need more to get the same effect. The sexual fantasy will need to become more and more exciting, leading to more provocative behavior. This need for more may lead your fantasy life into problems. (3) The way you achieve orgasm in masturbation involves a high level of stimulation that you could become conditioned to need in order to respond. This makes it more likely that you will become sexually frustrated with your partner because vaginal intercourse may not achieve that level of stimulation. (4) When masturbation is used to relieve stress or escape unpleasant feelings, it becomes a pattern of coping. That pattern becomes reinforced and works to take your mind off of the stress. This physical escape can become so habitual that other healthy ways of coping with stress are not explored or used. (5) Masturbation short-circuits the more sexually fulfilling union of two people who are joined as one flesh.

The Wired Sexual Revolution

As a national news contributor on mental health topics, I was called by a television network to discuss a headline about a wife who put a hit on her husband via text messaging. He had been unfaithful, and she was bent on revenge. In what seemed like a story line from a *CSI* episode, she ordered the hit, and the police used the text message as evidence in her arrest. Crazy, right? Welcome to the new frontier of relationships gone wild online.

This is just one of myriad relationship issues resulting from the new wired sexual revolution taking place in our culture. More common than jilted lovers using the internet to seek revenge is the alarming number of people electronically hooking up and forming liaisons with total strangers.

According to the *Journal of Couple and Relationship Therapy*,[21] approximately 50 percent of married women and 60 percent of married men will have an extramarital affair at some time in their marriage. What we don't know is when those affairs will happen—at the end of a failing relationship, during a marital crisis, or when opportunity presents itself. What we do know is that social media are providing more opportunities for infidelity.

While a large percentage of Americans still believe that extramarital affairs are wrong and are remaining faithful to their vows, infidelity is on the rise, especially among three groups: older men, young couples, and women. Older men now have access to more drugs and treatments that improve their physical health and enhance their sexuality. Younger couples' attitudes and perceptions of "normal" sexuality are being influenced by incessant mediated messages normalizing infidelity and easily accessed pornography online. More women engage in electronic affairs due to access and opportunity. A lonely housewife, for example, can seek admiration from an old flame on Facebook from the comfort of her kitchen while her child naps.

Furthermore, we have internet sites that do their best to reduce the stigma and the damage caused by affairs. Sites like AshleyMadison.com are dedicated to helping married spouses have discreet affairs. The site promotes itself as the leading dating service for married people, claiming to have twenty-three million customers in twenty-two countries who desire to cheat on their spouse.[22]

With news media reporting saucy stories of love in cyberspace, how widespread is online cheating? Catalogs.com's information library reports: [23]

- 57 percent of people use the internet to cheat.
- 38 percent of people have engaged in explicit online sexual conversations.
- 50 percent of people have talked on the phone with someone they first chatted with online.
- 31 percent of people have had an online conversation that has led to in-person sex.

One could easily wonder if cheating is inevitable given the amount of temptation encountered in a wired society. With more young people delaying marriage, increases in cohabitation rates, dating habits that include hookups, attempts to normalize pornography, and media determined to show casual sex with no consequences, there is an all-out assault on the words of Christ, "You have heard that it was said, 'Do not commit adultery.' But I tell you that anyone who looks at a woman lustfully has already committed adultery with her in his heart. If your right eye causes you to stumble, gouge it out and throw it away. It is better for you to lose one part of your body than for your whole body to be thrown into hell" (Matt. 5:27–29).

Sadly, too many people choose to ignore the biblical injunction to keep the marriage bed pure and instead decide to take their chances with God. Will he really judge adultery and sexual immorality? The prospect of cheap grace is often cited among believers who engage in online cheating. "God will forgive me." True, but the consequences could end a marriage and irreparably damage lives.

Social networking sites that connect former flames and allow users to make new friends online are being blamed for an increasing number of marital breakdowns. Talk to any divorce lawyer and they will tell you that the popularity of sites like Facebook and Bebo are tempting unhappy people to cheat. In fact, more and more of these sites are being used as legal evidence of affairs in divorce cases. For instance, when a sexual chat takes place online, it can be traced and retrieved by software designed to serve as an electronic private eye. Photos of spouses with their lovers posted online provide proof of an affair. And, publicly accessed text posts declaring love and affection can be used against a person who denies online involvement.

Mark Keenan, managing director of Divorce-Online, says this about divorce petitions: "I had heard from my staff that there were a lot of people saying they had found out things about their partners on Facebook and I decided to see how prevalent it was. I was really surprised to see 20 percent of all the petitions containing references to Facebook."[24] Divorce-Online also reported that in 2011, a third of all divorce filings had the word *Facebook* in them. Overall, the American Academy of Matrimonial Lawyers confirms that the use of social networking content is on the rise in divorce proceedings.[25]

Not only are social media public, but it's easy to access and laced with opportunity. Infidelity is often opportunity-driven. Thus, the temptation to boost your ego, feel appreciated, and satisfy temptation takes little convincing from those hurting in a relationship.

A 2008 Pew Internet and American Life Project survey found that about one in five adults uses Facebook to flirt.[26] Posts that become too intimate or tantalizing can quickly transform a trusted partner to a tempted one. Fast and easy emotional availability and regular communication with former friends and lovers can lead to affairs, both emotional and physical.

A 2008 study by Shackelford, Besser, and Goetz reported predictors of infidelity.[27] Those predictors included low conscientiousness and agreeability, impulsivity, and inability to delay. With so much opportunity at the click of a mouse or a tap of an app, it is easy to understand how those predictors are alive and well in the cyberworld of relationships. The normal stopgaps are gone.

Cyber relationships provide opportunity for quick intimacy and less inhibition. Take Harry, for example. He is hesitant to pick up the phone and call his lover at her home because her spouse might answer the phone. Instead he can privately message her and avoid immediate discovery.

So, how do we deal with the reality of cyber relationships and follow the words of the apostle Paul in Ephesians 5:3–5: "But among you there must not be even a hint of sexual immorality, or of any kind of impurity, or of greed, because these are improper for God's holy people. Nor should there be obscenity, foolish talk or coarse joking, which are out of place, but rather thanksgiving. For of this you can be sure: No immoral, impure or greedy person—such a man is an idolater—has any inheritance in the kingdom of Christ and of God." Safeguards must be in place to manage the temptation of online cheating.

Here are twenty guidelines that help keep you from cheating when it comes to social media:

1. Online activity needs to be discussed during a relationship. What is appropriate and what is not? What are the guardrails a couple needs to protect their relationship?
2. Have a guideline for friend requests. A good rule of thumb is to say no to any ex.
3. People tend to babble on social media and don't realize what they say is public and doesn't go away. Words must be chosen wisely.
4. Do not talk negatively about your partner online. If there was a fight, an upset, or a conflict, talk in person rather than announcing it to the cyberworld.
5. If secrets are kept, this is a red flag that the relationship is in trouble. Secrets are signs of deception.
6. Sexual intimacy is a private matter between spouses and should not be addressed in public forums like social media sites.
7. Don't confide in someone of the opposite sex about a marital problem. Even if a person is innocently looking for support, they are vulnerable to the attention of a good listener.
8. Let your partner know who contacted you, and if this poses a problem. This type of accountability will protect a marriage.

9. Make your communication clear so no unintended messages are sent. Remember, it is a human tendency to infer emotion to text-only messages.

10. Always judge your online communication by asking how your spouse would respond if they saw the post, chat, picture, or email. Emotional affairs begin with platonic friendships that become secret and intimate. Avoid private messaging and chatting.

11. Share passwords so that you can go on each other's social media sites.

12. Deactivate Facebook accounts when they cause relationship problems. If one partner is tempted, not managing time well, or spending more time with other people than the spouse, get rid of the temptation source.

13. If a spouse reconnects with someone from their past who wants to physically meet, drive with your spouse to the meeting or just say no.

14. Be the same person online that you are in person. It is easy to engage in fantasy and say things in the cyberworld that would not be said in person.

15. Work on the marriage offline. If the marriage is in trouble, go to counseling. Social media won't fix anything. Actually, more problems can be created. Cyber communications won't bring sizzle to a fizzled marriage.

16. Don't measure a spouse against some fantasy person online or start comparing posts from friends to a spouse. This can build negativity and lead to problems.

17. If someone of the opposite sex is flirting with you and becoming too intimate, hit the "unfriend" or "unfollow" option.

18. Watch the frequency of interactions with someone of the opposite sex. Think of it like this—if you went to lunch with that person every day and talked about your life, would a growing attraction emerge? Yes. Constant online conversation can do the same.

19. Limit time devoted to technology. So many people are jealous of the time a partner spends online and want their spouse back. Keep technology use in balance.
20. Celebrate marriage by writing positive and encouraging things to your spouse.

Navigating social media use and keeping abreast of its impact on relationships is a new frontier for most couples. Our wired world brings different challenges to the area of affairs and temptation. All couples must safeguard marriage by keeping God's Word at the center of marital life.

Because God created us in his image, both male and female, our differences often need to be better understood and discussed. Whatever is behind sexual conflicts in marriage, take responsibility for your part and commit to working on the physical relationship. As difficult as it is, talk about problems so you don't make wrong assumptions. Avoiding conversations about sexual issues only leads to resentment, growing apart, and possible betrayal.

One final suggestion to help deal with issues of sex and affection is to read through the Song of Solomon in the Bible as a couple. The book is a nuptial song that expresses love between a bride and her bridegroom. Whether you believe it is figurative or literal, it provides a healthy picture of attraction, love, affection, and the bond of consummated love.

After you read this poetic book of the Bible, ask yourself if you feel this way toward your spouse. If you can read those passages with tenderness toward your spouse, you are keeping love alive and may simply want to add a few of the suggestions in this chapter. If not, you need to spend time revisiting your relationship differences and do what needs to be done to reignite that spark.

11

Dealing with Difficult People

Conflict is inevitable, but combat is optional.

Max Lucado

For years, researchers have looked at how personality contributes to conflict styles and wondered why people respond differently to the same situations. For instance, why does someone react so intensely to an argument and others are able to maintain their cool? Or why is one person so irritable most of the time, and the other is easygoing? The answers have to do with personality. Personality differences can cause conflict. Sometimes people just don't get along because their personalities clash.

Conflict, then, is not based so much on an issue, but on who the person is and the patterns of behavior that have developed. When this is the case, problems can erupt anytime, anywhere.

When personalities clash, resolving conflict may not be as important as keeping the relationship intact. However, a challenging personality can make preserving the relationship a tough task.

The Making of a High-Conflict Person

Difficult people aren't born difficult. They become difficult through issues related to childhood attachments and years of making poor choices, blaming others, and having negative experiences often related to trauma and loss. They escalate conflict and operate in ways that make it difficult to ever resolve issues. In fact, they usually *create* drama.

Eben Gossage was one of those people. He wanted to practice law in the state of California. After completing law school and passing the California bar exam, he was denied. The Committee of Bar Examiners found him lacking in what they called good moral character.

Eben appealed his case to the State Bar Court. This court ruled in his favor, recommending that he be admitted to the practice of law. However, the California Supreme Court decided to review his case and once again ruled against him. Their decision rested on the facts of his case. Those facts suggested a negative pattern of behavior. They didn't feel Eben was fit to practice law.

This is Eben's story.

According to public record,[1] Eben was the son of a prominent advertising executive in the San Francisco Bay area. He and his younger sister, Amy, were little when their parents divorced. When Eben was around age fifteen, his father died. What followed was a life of drinking and using illicit drugs. Eben's heroin habit was costly and he stole money to support his habit. Eventually, he dropped out of school and lived off of the inherited money from his father and grandfather.

During his drugging days, Eben was convicted of a felony for forgery that led to probation. He continued to have drug problems and pled guilty to two more felony counts while on probation. The judge remanded Eben to drug treatment before sentencing, but Eben was uncooperative and landed in custody. During that time, his mother died.

Upon his release from custody, the unemployed Eben started to use and drink again. Still on probation for forgery, he visited his sister, became violent during his visit, and killed her. According to the record, Eben repeatedly hit his sister with a hammer, did not get help for her once he realized what he had done, repeatedly stabbed her, fled the scene, and concealed his guilt. He was arrested and charged with murder but was convicted of voluntary manslaughter. He spent two and a half years in the state prison and then was paroled. His drug use resumed. He violated his parole and pled guilty to reckless driving.

In and out of jail, Eben admitted guilt to a DUI (after he failed to report to court the first time) that led to probation and agreed to attend an alcohol awareness program. Later, he stole jewelry from a family friend who tried to help him. Two years later, he was charged with possession of heroin and other misdemeanors. More charges were added to his record, and the pattern continued until he was finally sent to state prison. There he claimed his life changed.

Again, paroled, Eben sobered up, entered college and eventually law school, and passed the bar exam the first time he took it. For years after his release, Eben helped nonprofit groups in urban redevelopment, lobbied public officials and agencies regarding pollution problems, volunteered in local political campaigns, helped drug-addicted youths, and more. A list of impressive people testified to the change they believed took place in Eben's life. Eben appeared to be sober, honest, and remorseful for his life of drug abuse and the killing of his sister.

While he appeared to be a model citizen after his release from prison, he did ignore minor traffic violations that he accumulated. He had numerous vehicle violations that required his appearance in court, but he failed to appear. Finally, after years, he paid all his outstanding traffic violations. Six months after his bills were paid, he applied to the Committee of Bar Examiners for a moral character determination in order to practice law. He downplayed his problems on his application and failed to report every minor violation. Furthermore, answers on his application were incomplete, yet he signed the application and declared he truthfully completed the questions.

At his hearing, Eben presented twenty lay witnesses who attested to his change in character and sobriety. Five mental health professionals interviewed Eben. They testified that he was completely rehabilitated, free from substance abuse or personality disorders. But one witness for the committee could not reconcile the traffic violations. He thought these violations and failure to report all of his criminal record indicated an antisocial attitude or personality disorder. He saw a pattern of misconduct that others missed or justified because of Eben's sobriety and good works. In his opinion, there was no period in Eben's life when he lived by the rule of the law.

The California Supreme Court needed a compelling show of reform to recommend Eben and did not feel they had one based on the traffic violations and application omissions. Eben had continued to break the law and refused to conform to the rules. This, to the court, suggested a lack of respect for the law. Thus, his petition was denied and he could not practice law.

The case against Eben rested on a continuing pattern of behavior. People like Eben have deeply embedded ways of thinking and behaving that create what we call personality disorders. People with personality disorders exhibit long-standing patterns of behavior that make them difficult to trust or be around. Their personality patterns are deeply ingrained and difficult to change.

Behind all the drama is usually someone who has serious issues with attachment from childhood. Experiences lead them to develop a mistrust of others and/or they don't cope well with loss, fears of abandonment, feeling inferior, being dominated by others, or being ignored. They keep people at arm's length because people cause pain.

Characteristics of High-Conflict People

High-conflict people are people whose patterns of behavior make conflict worse rather than better. Conflict is usually viewed as a personal assault. Typically, their thinking is rigid and emotions are not managed. They react in extreme ways and blame others, not exactly the necessary traits for working things out.

Characteristics of a high-conflict person include blaming others, avoiding responsibility for any part of a problem, all-or-nothing thinking, seeking attention and allies, dramatic and emotional appeals, lying because of desperation, bringing up the past, and looking to punish those who have hurt them.

Thought Patterns of the High-Conflict Person

Thinking for the high-conflict person is often an all-or-nothing process. Everything is black and white, good or bad. Other points of view are not considered, and high-conflict people must have their way. Compromise is not an option because it feels like losing. Whatever the person feels at the moment is true for them.

Rigid thinking blocks the person from looking for simple solutions or compromise. Because they aren't flexible and tend to see things in all-or-nothing terms, working through conflict becomes one-sided—their way or the highway!

Emotions of the High-Conflict Person

The emotions of the high-conflict person are intense and are used to manipulate, making conflict resolution or rational conversation difficult. Emotion is the primary way they use to charm others and get sympathy.

High-conflict people often have excessive anger that is related to past disappointments and issues of emotional neglect. It shows up in relationships through poor impulse control, impaired thoughts, and reactivity. Anger is used to influence, to keep people away, and to control. Many can't handle their anger in an appropriate way and don't admit to angry feelings. For example, someone who needs to be the center of attention may channel anger into body complaints of an eating disorder or substance abuse. If anger can be uncovered and acknowledged, there is more of a chance for progress, even forgiveness.

Actions of the High-Conflict Person

Actions and consequences are not connected. Extreme action follows intense emotions—yelling, controlling, saying disrespectful things, giving the silent treatment, spreading rumors, hitting, stalking, threatening if you don't agree, and lying.

High-conflict people push others away, sabotaging their desire for satisfying relationships. Most of this is driven by not wanting to lose control, thus, the high-conflict person tries to control and dominate. Blaming leads to feeling stronger and creates a false sense of safety.

The problem with difficult people is that they don't look at their own behavior but instead play the blame game. Much energy goes into attacking others rather than reflecting on their own actions. This enduring pattern makes conflict resolution difficult because they are not looking to solve problems. Rather, they look for advocates in the blame process. Who can they get on their side so they can avoid any self-blame or responsibility?

If you question a high-conflict person during a disagreement, you will encounter escalation, drama, manipulation, and a loose grip of the facts.

High-Conflict and Personality Disorders

Not all high-conflict people have a personality disorder, but many do. Personality disorders develop due to a combination of factors—genetic vulnerability or temperament, childhood trauma, verbal abuse, and high reactivity.

Childhood attachment is often characterized by the neglect of the child's emotional needs, although how big a role this plays is still unknown. It is believed that insecure or disrupted childhood attachment is a factor. Even though parenting behavior plays a role, parents are not necessarily to blame. Additional influences like high sensitivity or temperament make these kids more dramatic and disruptive. Teens often have conduct problems, anxiety, and depression as well. Healthy coping strategies are missing, identity suffers, and family interactions become problematic. Conflict is not worked out in ways that are healthy. Negative patterns develop.

Think of people with personality disorders as having blind spots when it comes to reflecting on their behavior. Their problems keep repeating, but they don't recognize the patterns or make changes. Instead, they continue in self-defeating ways and distance people in relationships. Worse, they blame and persuade others to be their advocates of blame.

A strong relationship with a friend, relative, teacher, or meaningful person can offset negative influences. A loving grandmother or teacher can make a difference. So can life events. However, when personality and life events come together in a negative way, the development of a personality disorder can be triggered. Once negative patterns are developed, working through conflict becomes treacherous.

In general, controlling anger and learning to forgive helps high-conflict people in their relationships. Humanly, this is difficult, but when the hig-conflict person invites the Holy Spirit to participate in his life, there is hope for true change to take place. Conflicts can be worked on and reconciliation is possible.

Living with a High-Conflict Person

While Eben Gossage represents the extreme of a difficult person, most of us have a few difficult people in our lives. At times, we feel at a loss as to how to bring up problems without things ending poorly. Their instability, potential for harm, or constant refusal to take responsibility frustrates and scares us. Yet, when those difficult people are in our lives, we have to engage them and know how to handle conflict.

Now that you have a picture of what you are dealing with in high-conflict relationships, it is important to respond in ways that don't escalate conflict. Here are general guidelines. It is a long list. There is much to remember so you may want to think about a difficult person in your life and apply one or two of these guidelines at a time.

1. *Don't tell the person that they are high-conflict or have a personality disorder.* Labeling backfires. Instead, concentrate on ways to better manage your relationship. Since the high-conflict person struggles with connection, you will need to be the one who listens and shows empathy and respect. Doing this will lower the person's defenses, making room for the beginning of trust. Labeling or pointing out the person's faults escalates rage and irrationality.

2. *Don't fight back or try to prove how correct you are.* This doesn't work. The person will try to find allies to defend their position and continue to battle.

3. *Try to stay calm.* When the emotion intensifies, say something like, "We can revisit this when we are both calmer." The person in the conflict can own part of the problem, rather than singling out the high-conflict person for being so unreasonable. Remember that the intense mood belongs to the other person. Don't engage on that level or it will become a contest.

4. *Assess your safety.* If there are dangerous behaviors like domestic violence or behaviors that could be fatal to the relationship, for example, serial infidelity or out-of-control spending, then you need to make sure you are safe and controls are in place. Other than that, the goal with high-conflict people is to reduce conflict.

5. *Relate to the person around tasks that need to be done or possible solutions rather than reacting to their emotions.* Emotions distract from the issue at hand, so keep the issue front and center. Focus only on behavior. Think like a detective:

"Just the facts." Trying to work through emotions usually leads to more blame.

6. *Choose your battles.* Since most high-conflict people love the battle, minimize your contact with that person when you can. When you do engage, resist the urge to defend yourself, which only ends in more conflict.

7. *Set a structure for conflict discussion and talk about expectations.* Establish rules for fair fighting, such as no yelling, name-calling, interrupting, etc. It may help to meet in a public place to keep emotions in check.

8. *Keep emotions from intensifying so people can think and talk sensibly.* Begin a conflict by saying something like, "I understand your frustrations. I am paying attention to how you feel and what you say. Let's see if we can come up with a solution." Or respond by saying, "You may be right," or "Tell me more about that." This eliminates push back and keeps the emotion level down.

9. *Set boundaries.* You will be tempted to bend your boundaries in order to keep the emotions down, but this will only backfire. If a boundary is violated, be firm. Tell the person what the expectation is and what is needed to continue the conversation. Although you may want to, don't ignore the person. Ignoring usually sets the person up for even more anger because it triggers feelings of emotional neglect and abandonment. Better to revisit the rules of engagement.

10. *Disengage from the drama and manage your own thoughts and feelings.* When someone starts accusing you and using *always* or *never* in the conversation, disengage and realize this will go nowhere. Take a time-out or concentrate on your reaction only.

11. *Make a decision not to bring in outside allies to support your position.* Conflict is not about convincing the other person that you are right. It is about listening to each other and coming to a solution. So don't agree to bring in advocates

or allies unless you need a mediator. Avoid the triangle—bringing in a third party to deal with a conflict between two people.

12. *Do reality testing.* You can't challenge a person's perception directly because the conflict will escalate, emotion will take over, and nothing will get solved. But you can ask questions in a more *indirect* way. Say something like, "Sometimes people get really angry at others when they are hurt and want to make them pay. Do you know what I mean?" This is indirect but will keep the conversation going and help you discern whether the person is intentionally trying to deceive you to get what they want, or whether there really is a distortion in the way they think. Chances are that everything the person says isn't a lie or exaggeration. Parts may be true. And they may believe what they said to you, so don't assume the person is lying or exaggerating. Check it out.

13. *Be patient.* In my experience, working on conflict with a difficult person takes time and patience. Change is often slow but can happen with commitment to the process and desire to work on the relationship. The person has to experience calmer approaches and see that working through issues can be done and accomplishes more than acting in extreme ways.

14. *Talk about the elements of a healthy relationship.* Healthy relationships have similar characteristics—respect for one another, support, empathy, sharing thoughts and feelings without fear of negativity, mutual trust, honesty, and fidelity. In healthy relationships, people like to spend time together and try to be fair and grow in connection and intimacy over time. Healthy relationships are not characterized by blaming, criticizing, idealizing, projecting, raging, embarrassing, demeaning, yelling, lying, and always being right. Helping the person see that certain behaviors make a person more interpersonally effective is one goal.

15. *The most effective psychotherapy is called dialectical behavior therapy (DBT).* This therapy helps people learn to calm

down and soothe themselves, tolerate distress, develop coping skills, and learn how to be more interpersonally effective. For whatever reasons, people with personality disorders are deeply wounded people. With slow and steady help, they can learn to be more effective in dealing with conflict in relationships, but it may take a professional mental health therapist to move them forward. Be willing to include yourself in treatment so you can work together on finding ways to effectively deal with conflict. Don't bring up the idea of treatment in the middle of a fight. Wait until things are calm and then suggest help for the two of you in order to work together.

When there is a difficult person in your life, think about what triggers the conflict. Is there something the person does or a habit that makes you crazy? Maybe it is a look, a smart remark, or a constant goading you into arguments. More importantly, is there some topic, situation, or cue that sets this person off? For example, if every time you bring up a political topic, the person escalates, that is probably a subject you want to avoid.

In terms of keeping conflict to a minimum, it is best to stay as neutral as possible and not give too many opinions. If the person continues to try to engage you in conflict, make an excuse to do something else or simply say, "I would rather not get in to this."

If you find yourself in a conflict, avoid using the "b" word (but) when you respond. The "but . . ." seems to negate what the other person says. Then the difficult person doesn't feel heard and may escalate.

You can exit the conflict if things are escalating, but make sure you do it by telling the person you care about them and want to hear what they have to say. Say something like, "When we talk, it has to be respectful, so a time-out for both of us to calm down may be a good idea."

If the person becomes hostile or verbally abusive, confront calmly and be specific about the behavior. Tell the person to stop bullying or demeaning you and to talk about the issue without the abuse. Emotion is overruling logic, so bring the person back to logic—stop yelling and we can talk. Be specific about the behavior. If abuse iṣ in the picture, see a therapist and talk about the possibility of retaliation. Safety is a concern, and the high-conflict person needs to know that there will be consequences for abusive behavior.

Remember that in a high-conflict situation, the only part you control is your reaction. Say as little as possible. Stay calm and don't try to reason with the person. Don't try to explain yourself because a difficult person doesn't empathize with you. Think about the Southern saying, "You catch more flies with honey than vinegar." This applies to difficult people. Staying positive, especially in your tone, diffuses the fight.

What If *I* Am the High-Conflict Person?

If you are reading this and thinking, *Maybe I am the difficult person*, then begin to work on your reactions. Think about what sets you off. Do you place demands on other people? Are they realistic? Do you struggle when people don't make you feel good? Are you easily irritated over minor things? Do you need a time-out to calm down and rethink your reactions?

People let us down all the time. If we look to others to boost our esteem or find our identity, we will be disappointed on a regular basis. That disappointment can lead to anger and upset and a constant feeling of being let down. Thus, we have to learn to put our trust in God, not people. This means looking to God for esteem and identity.

You are highly esteemed by God because he created and chose you. Nothing you do changes this fact. Accepting God's love and allowing it to change you is the first step to becoming less difficult. God's love is transforming. He can soften the feelings of abandonment and rejection. He promises to never do either in a relationship with you. Yes, you may still go through difficult times, but his love is never withdrawn and his Spirit lives in you if you become one of his children.

You reflect his image. God wants you to have a healthy view of yourself in order to then love others. Our esteem comes from being one of his. This means that no matter your background or troubled relationships, God's love can heal those places of hurt.

When you have a personal relationship with Jesus, you can be secure in who you are. Psalm 34:4 says we can be free of all fears. Psalm 55:22 tells us that God will never allow us to be shaken to the point of not being able to cope. Psalm 91 reminds us that God rescues and protects us from harm. Isaiah 54:17 tells us that no weapon formed against us will prosper. John 10:28 encourages us that we are secure in our faith and nothing can separate us from God's love. Finally, the hope to change can be found in Philippians 1:6—the good work that God began in us will be completed. It may be helpful to work with a Christian therapist who can help you find this security in Christ.

The Challenge to Love

Perhaps the Serenity Prayer is a good reminder when we interact with difficult people. We need the serenity to accept the things we cannot change, and the courage to change the things we can (me!). Most of all, we need wisdom to not escalate problems and remain compassionate for the person who struggles so desperately.

Jesus challenges us with his command to love our neighbor. Our neighbor can be difficult. Our neighbor can mow his lawn and throw grass all over our car. Our neighbor can gossip about us and be passive-aggressive. Our neighbor can blame us for all her problems or walk away from issues when they come to a head. Our neighbor can have a personality disorder.

The love Jesus calls us to is a love that led him to die on the cross for people who were more than unkind to him. He went to hell to keep us out of it! His command to love our neighbor includes those with whom we clash and those who can be difficult. This is not an easy road, but love is the only road that takes us to where we need to go.

12

><-

Anger and Resentment

If the only tool you have is a hammer, you tend to treat everything as if it were a nail.

Abraham Maslow

Our story begins in the office of a prominent divorce attorney. A distraught client is determined to divorce his wife and seeks the attorney's help. The attorney listens to his client's woes and tells him something rather startling. He is about to waive his $450 an hour fee because the advice he has is so important that he wants to give it for free. Still unable to shake the tragic plight of his friends, Oliver and Barbara Rose, he begins to tell their story in the hope that it will make this man rethink his desire for a divorce.

The attorney's friend, Oliver Rose, married Barbara, a gymnast whom he met while at Harvard Law School. Oliver and Barbara met at an auction and shared a love for exquisite possessions. Love came quickly and they soon married. Oliver became a partner in his law firm, and Barbara devoted her time and energy to making a home by restoring an old mansion and enjoying the financial success of Oliver's law career. The couple had two children and, by all accounts, appeared to have the perfect marriage. But appearances can be deceiving.

Seventeen years of marriage passed, and Barbara grew restless and began to have doubts about her marriage. At times, she fantasized about what her life would be like without Oliver and liked the idea. She began to find fault with her husband, harboring a growing dislike for him. That dislike grew into stronger feelings of dislike. Eventually, she felt contempt for her husband.

Oliver, not understanding why Barbara felt the way she did, didn't pay attention to the growing relationship problems. He failed to recognize the impact of his self-centeredness and dismissive attitude toward his wife. The two argued more and more, creating major strain in the marriage. Conflict characterized the marriage.

After one harrowing argument, Oliver thought he was having a heart attack. To his relief, this was not true, and he was diagnosed with a hiatal hernia. Thinking Oliver could have died, Barbara realized she no longer loved her husband and showed no concern for him. In fact, she would have felt relieved by his death. She decided to admit to these feelings and asked Oliver for a divorce.

Even though Oliver agreed to the divorce, tension mounted and conflict grew. Neither wanted to leave the well-appointed house. The couple fought over the house and everything in it and tried to force the other out. At one point, Barbara threw Oliver out of the house, but he returned on a legal loophole he found in the divorce agreement. The couple's conflict crescendoed to an all-time high, both determined to hurt the other in as many ways as possible.

Escalating anger led to regular humiliation of the other and destruction of household items. Barbara crashed Oliver's antique car on purpose; Oliver ran over her cat in the driveway; Barbara trapped Oliver in their in-home sauna, where he almost died from heat stroke and dehydration. The destructive behavior continued as the two displayed their contemptuous feelings for one another.

When the kids went off to college, Oliver tried to make peace, but the contempt was by then so powerful that it escalated to more physical destruction. All civility had been lost.

The story peaked during a final showdown in which Oliver physically attacked Barbara, who fled to the attic. Later, she loosened the chandelier in an attempt to drop it on Oliver to kill him. The verbal sparring escalated. The couple climbed the chandelier to physically get at each other. As they hung precariously on the loosened chandelier, there appeared to be no resolution to the bitterness between them. But during a contemplative moment, Oliver admitted that despite all, he still loved Barbara.

Just when you thought Barbara might come around, and maybe the hate would subside, she rebuffed him. The chandelier could no longer support their weight, and the couple crashed to the ground. In one final gesture before each succumbed to death from the fall, Oliver reached for Barbara's hand to hold it. Barbara bitterly knocked Oliver's hand away, refusing him to the end. The conflict ended with the couple lying dead on the floor of their opulent mansion.

At the end of the story, the divorce attorney turns to his client who has come for a divorce, and offers two options: continue with his nasty divorce or go home and work on the problems in his marriage. After hearing the horrific story of two people whose love turned to hatred, the man leaves the divorce attorney's office and decides to give his marriage another try. It was too late for Oliver and Barbara Rose, but maybe his marriage could be saved.

The above story, *The War of the Roses*, is based on the 1981 book by Warren Adler adapted for film. It graphically depicts a vicious divorce battle in which two people could not work out their differences and became enemies. The portrayal of a happily married couple's descent into darkness is tragic as we witness the consequences of one spouse deciding she would be better off without the other. Conflict escalates to the worst possible level. The relationship war ends in a battle with no victory.

The reality of conflict gone wild stares us in the face, and it is ugly. Who wants a battle with no victory? The anger, the bitterness, the hatred, the need to be right, and the refusal to deal with differences end in destruction. We witness the worst side of unresolved conflict.

While most of us are not in this type of angry relationship, we still feel the occasional sting of conflict gone bad—confrontations that end with lingering negativity. Differences that aren't discussed. Long-standing battles that sap our energy. At those times, we wish conflict would magically disappear.

As Oliver and Barbara show us, uncontrolled anger is dangerous. It not only destroys relationships but also destroys people. Left untouched, anger and unforgiveness fester to the point of boiling. This is why the Bible is so clear on how to handle anger and unforgiveness. God's intention is to keep our hearts from hardening and to prevent a war of the roses.

Anger Unleashed

On February 26, 2012, George Zimmerman, a neighborhood watch captain of a gated community in Sanford, Florida, called 911 to report a "suspicious person" walking in the neighborhood. He was told not to approach the person or get out of his SUV, but he did. What happened next is unclear. There was a struggle and a gunshot. A teenager, Trayvon Martin, was dead. Zimmerman was bleeding from his nose and the back of his head but survived the altercation.

Zimmerman was charged with second-degree murder and stood trial. The defense for Zimmerman rested on reasonable doubt. Away from the courthouse, the case became a race relations touchpoint, tried in the media. George is multiracial (Hispanic and white) and Trayvon was African-American.

On July 13, 2013, the jury found Zimmerman not guilty. The verdict further fueled racial tensions. Police worried about riots in the streets. People were angry and threatening violence. The case became an event that divided America along racial lines.

Dr. Alveda King, niece of Dr. Martin Luther King Jr., joined the public conversation and reminded us of her uncle's words—we must all learn to live together as brothers and sisters or perish as fools.[1] She called for nonviolence as a reaction to the verdict and challenged us to not overlook the daily murders in our streets.

Every day people die at the hands of each other over conflict and strife. Nonviolent conflict resolution is desperately needed. Most people would agree. Anger can be a dangerous weapon. Violence, however, is not a solution. Yet, our culture continues to show violence and revenge as responses to anger.

Anger can be positive when it is used as a signal to tell us that something is wrong or is a plea for justice. In relationships, anger is a cue to articulate our need or tell someone what is frustrating us. When expressed properly, it can be a constructive emotion. When anger is not handled in a healthy way, it damages relationships. Left unchecked, it can lead us to break or hit things, name-call, intimidate, put people down, and act out in violence. When anger is expressed destructively, it intensifies conflict.

Anger is a powerful emotion. That is why it needs to be controlled. When we get angry, our heart rate increases, our muscles tense, our blood pressure rises, and we are aroused. We feel alive, maybe even exhilarated.

The momentary good we feel dissipates quickly. Instead of bringing closeness, anger alienates those we care about. Anger and bitterness are like viruses that work their way through our lives, infecting others.

Repressing Anger

Because you can't separate the mind and body, holding on to anger disrupts feelings of well-being. What you feel and believe impacts your physical health. In fact, repressed anger activates stress hormones and makes us more prone to illness.[2]

Repressed anger is when you feel anger but do not acknowledge or express it. You may have learned this behavior growing up. Maybe you were told not to get angry. Maybe your parents repressed their anger because they didn't want you to be afraid. Whatever the case, anger behavior is learned.

Repressed anger builds up and leads to resentment. Dr. Theodore Rubin, a New York psychoanalyst, believes repressed anger is the source of much anxiety. In his book, *The Angry Book*, he talks about repressed anger as a major root of anxiety disorders.[3]

Dana knows about repressing anger. She came to therapy for depression, but anger was at the root of her problem.

One day Dana had caught her husband in the act of viewing pornography. He denied it. However, when she did a little digging, she found a trail of pornography.

Dana knew her husband lied and was living a secret life but said she was not angry. Yet her stomach hurt every day. She complained of headaches. All that negative energy associated with hidden anger was causing her to feel physical pain.

One of Dana's church friends noticed how restless Dana seemed to be and asked if everything was all right. Dana thanked her for her concern and said, "Yes, I'm fine. Don't worry. God is good." She certainly didn't want anyone to know what was going on in her household. It was important to act like she had it all together. Maybe she was making too much out of her discoveries. Maybe it was only a few times her husband looked at porn and it would all blow over.

Dana continued to stuff the anger. This was her way of maintaining control. If she admitted anger, her husband might leave or blow up at her. Her marriage would be a mess. To prevent feeling bad, she repressed her anger and prayed it would all go away.

A few weeks later, Dana caught her husband again and blew up, a normal response to repressed anger. But she was surprised by her reaction. So we talked about what led up to the explosion. What were the signs that anger was lurking under the surface?

First, Dana was restless about the pornography issue. Even though she didn't admit to being angry, she wasn't happy with herself or her husband. Something was stirring in her. Things were not quite right.

Second, she began to find fault with her husband. She found herself picking on him for small things and judging every action. When anger is denied, it can leak out in passive-aggressive ways.

Third, she was moody. When her husband asked her what was wrong, she said, "Nothing." He could tell she was irritable and unhappy. Dana directed the anger to herself, creating depression. This anger turned inward was at the root of Dana's depression. She was really angry with her husband for lying and betraying her.

Fourth, the anger was building. Every day, Dana felt more and more out of control. She had thoughts of hurting her husband, exposing him, getting revenge, or retaliating. She wanted him to pay for his lies and the hurt he was causing her.

Fifth, she didn't know what to do and began to feel hopeless. Her husband denied a serious problem that affected their marriage, and she was feeling like there was no solution. This was feeding the depression.

I explained to Dana that repressing anger is a temporary solution and one that was causing her physical and emotional problems. She had a choice. She could carry the anger around and pretend it wasn't there or she could tell the truth. But she could do this on her terms, when she felt prepared and ready. This was real control.

She chose to admit to the anger and develop a strategy to deal with her husband's denial and lies. When she did, her stomach stopped hurting and her mood improved. Once she was able to talk about her anger, she calmed down. The hurt and sadness of the betrayal hit her hard, but she no longer carried the burden of pretending and stuffing the anger inside.

Venting Anger

Years ago, when I first became a therapist, it was popular for therapists to give angry couples a type of foam bat and tell them to go ahead and hit each other in order to vent their anger. The bats couldn't physically hurt anyone, and the idea was to get out all the rage and anger.

We applied this idea to angry teenagers as well—telling parents to encourage their teens to pound on pillows or a punching bag. Again, the prescriptions were based on the idea that venting anger releases it.

Then came Primal Scream therapy in which clients were asked to regress to the moment of birth and scream against all the rage that comes from leaving that safe place of the womb—let me say this was not a mainstream treatment and not one I ever recommended! But the notion of the bats and the screaming was the same. Vent your anger in order to let it go.

Because repressed anger causes all kinds of physical maladies like heart attacks, headaches, overeating, depression, and colitis, the more you could get out that festering anger the better, right?

Wrong. Venting anger doesn't work. It just fans the flames. Anger is actually more destructive when it is full-on expressed. Expression releases the same hormones that are produced under stress and does damage to the body. A hostile attitude may even lead to heart disease, according to Duke researcher Dr. Redford Williams.[4] Intense anger wreaks havoc on the body.

Feeling angry is one thing, but letting it all out in unchecked ways is worse than repression. Venting damages relationships. Giving someone a piece of your mind can destroy the rest of the pieces of the relationship!

A man hits his wife; a woman slaps her child. An angry driver shouts out the window of a car. A first-class passenger takes a swing at the flight attendant who wouldn't move his bag. A worker snaps and shoots his co-workers. Anger, left unchecked, can turn destructive like it did in the Zimmerman-Martin case.

Jeremy knows this but struggles to express anger in a way that doesn't hurt people. "I don't know what comes over me. It's the littlest things that irritate me. Then, I explode. It doesn't matter who is with me. My anger gets unleashed, and I feel terrible. I tell myself I won't do that again. But I do."

People like Jeremy are easily aroused to anger. Noise, crowds, frustration, low tolerance, and aggressive activities don't necessarily create anger, but they can arouse it. In a state of physical arousal, minor things become major and trigger anger.

The Anger Quiz

Maybe you don't know how angry you are, or if you are carrying anger around. Maybe your ideas about anger are based on false ideas like the venting idea. Take this short quiz and see how well you understand anger. Answer true or false to each question.

1. As long as I don't look or sound angry, I'm not.
2. If I ignore anger long enough, it will go away.
3. If I punch something or throw something, I will feel less angry.
4. Anger is shameful and not part of a healthy person.
5. It is okay to keep the peace. That is what God wants.
6. If I express anger, my relationships will be in danger.
7. Women don't get angry, just upset.
8. Christians should not get angry.
9. God understands that sometimes I just lose control.
10. As long as I didn't mean to get angry, it's okay.

If you answered true to *any* of these questions, take a second look at the question. All the answers are false. Anger is easily misunderstood. It is a signal to pay attention to what is going on around you or inside you. It is not a sin to feel anger, but we can sin in the way we express anger.

Anger Triggers

Even Freud realized that catharsis of anger doesn't work and encouraged people to look at *why* they got angry. And while I don't always agree with Freud's ideas, he was on the right track here. If you feel angry, you need to get at the cause. What provokes you?

Anger is triggered by expectations, perceptions, and things people say and do. Specific things said or done create hot buttons for anger—those triggers that cause the feeling to rise.

Knowing your hot buttons can prepare you for future conflicts. For example, a hot button in Andy's relationship with his brother has to do with jokes about height. Andy is smaller and shorter than his brother. All his life, Andy's brother has relentlessly teased him about being short. Andy has had enough, and the jokes are an ongoing source of conflict.

To deal with hot buttons, think about how you respond. Is your response effective in keeping you calm and dealing with the problem? If not, you may have to change your reaction. To do this, focus on what you do or say that might keep the anger going or calm it down. Only notice what the other person is doing so you can identify what sets you off. Then, think about what you want to accomplish for the moment. For example, do you want to be less angry, calmer, or more able to respond to negativity without blowing up?

In Andy's case, his goal was to not let his brother's jokes get to him. Andy valued the relationship he had with his brother, but the joking was wearing away the good feelings. Andy's repeated attempts at asking his brother to stop hadn't worked. Getting mad didn't work either. Andy needed a new strategy.

Andy decided to react with indifference to the jokes. He wondered if his anger fueled his brother's joking even more. If he changed his reaction, the joking might stop. And in reality, he only had control over his reactions anyway.

The next time Andy's brother made a joke, Andy looked his

brother in the eye and calmly said, "Is that the best you have?" His brother tried again. But Andy maintained his cool. "Old joke, bro!"

After weeks of Andy remaining cool and calm, his brother finally gave up. There was no fun in not getting a reaction from Andy. It worked. The joking stopped. Remaining calm and matter-of-fact was the key to change.

So imagine you are eating at a family dinner and that annoying uncle makes another smart remark to you with the intent to upset you. What can you do?

Hope he stops? Well, he hasn't for years, so that probably won't be the case. Ignore him? You could try, but past experience says he will keep it up until he sees you lose it. Get upset and try to change him? Yes, this is where most of us live, even though it rarely works. Work on your reaction? Bingo! This is the part we control.

Sometimes you can avoid anger hot buttons completely. If certain situations or people cue anger, and those people are not important in your life, you can avoid them or the situation. For example, you can avoid drinking if that arouses anger. You can avoid playing in a basketball league if losing sets you off. You can avoid a neighbor who insults you. You can avoid that obnoxious co-worker. In these cases, avoidance is like avoiding temptation—don't put yourself with people or into situations that will trigger your anger if it isn't necessary. This strategy doesn't get at the root of the anger problem, but it will help you maintain your cool.

Ways to Calm Down

Once you know your hot buttons, pay attention to the physical signs in your body that tell you that you are getting angry—heart rate and muscle tension, for example. Andy could feel the anger coursing through his body when his brother joked on him. He knew he had to learn to regulate that intensity.

Andy did what others do—found ways to soothe and calm his body. Here is a list of strategies.

1. Take a few deep breaths. Slow breathing is incompatible with stress and calms down the body.
2. Count to ten and pause so you don't react impulsively.
3. Focus your thoughts on a neutral object in the room.
4. Think of something positive in the moment or pray.
5. Relax your muscles by tensing and then relaxing them. This is called progressive or deep muscle relaxation and can be practiced during non-conflict times and then used when you feel angry.
6. Think on things that are good—a biblical prescription (see Phil. 4:8).
7. Refuse to be easily offended.
8. Exercise so stress and anger have an outlet.
9. Establish anger rules so conflict doesn't disintegrate into blame and shouting.
10. Use humor to break tension.

When you are calm, tell the person what you are feeling, but remember to use "I" statements and not blame. Andy might say to his brother, "You know, I don't find those size jokes funny. Actually, they hurt me so please stop." Before Andy learned to press pause on his anger and get control, he lashed back, only escalating the conflict further.

For some people, the ability to calm down is challenging. They are literally flooded with emotion that kicks in their hormones and raises the pulse, heart rate, and other stress reactions. They literally feel flooded by the emotion. During this time of flooding, they can't think straight because they are warding off stress. Then they attack.

In order to control anger in relationships, the source of anger is important to determine as well. *Situational anger* is anger that rises up in response to words or actions. It is helpful to work through situational anger when it happens and not let it build.

Chronic anger is another story. It often stems from years of hurt, neglect, abuse, or trauma. Chronic anger is more difficult to work on because of the years of hurt involved. When a hot button is hit, anger is unleashed. But the hot button is often not in a person's awareness.

What Does Anger Do for You?

One of the reasons we hold on to anger even when it wreaks havoc in our relationships is because we think it works for us. We don't like to give up things that serve a purpose. So ask yourself, "What does anger do for me?"

Is it motivated by some deficiency or a reflexive response to unfair treatment? We hold on to the belief that life must be fair in order to cope with the fact that it is not. When we continue to believe and act like life must be fair, we collect a rich supply of injustices that only fuel anger. But will anger bring me the results I desire—reconciliation, growth, better relationships, and fulfillment in life? Not usually.

Sometimes anger serves the purpose of self-pity. Anger is a strategy to manipulate others to feel sorry for us, so we complain and hassle people. This backfires in that people don't want to be around complainers or someone who is full of self-pity.

Anger also serves the purpose of covering vulnerability. Rather than showing the "weaker" side of our emotional lives, we use anger to appear strong. Under the anger may be a story of hurt or pain. Letting go means being vulnerable. And we don't want to feel vulnerable.

Anger is also a simple solution to more complex relationship issues. Being angry is a very narrow and rigid way to respond to issues that take time and thought to process and work through. Anger is easy. Working through problems is more difficult.

In order to let go of anger, identify the function anger serves. Is it healthy? Does it help your relationships? If you let go of anger, what would you feel instead?

Holding a Grudge

A grudge involves holding resentment because of some real or imagined wrong. A grudge develops when you don't like the way a conflict ended. Nursing a grudge can lead to revenge. Consider the story of John the Baptist in Mark 6 of the Bible.

Herod was a tetrarch under the Roman Empire. He fell in love with his brother's wife, Herodias, who was also his niece. Herodias agreed to marry Herod if he would divorce his first wife. Talk about family conflict!

John the Baptist was a rather outspoken prophet who criticized Herod for this marriage. Herod wasn't happy about the judgment and imprisoned John. He would have killed John but was afraid of how the people would respond to the killing of one of their prophets. Herod wanted to avoid an uprising.

Herodias was angry that John called her marriage unlawful. She held this against John and nursed the grudge. She was so angry that she looked for an opportunity to have John killed.

In the story, Herod has a birthday party. Herodias's daughter dances and pleases the tetrarch. Because Herod was so pleased, he tells the daughter to ask anything she likes and he will give it to her. Having been coached by her mother, the daughter asks for the head of John the Baptist, thus securing her mother's revenge. This biblical story would have ended differently had Herod listened to the truth, accepted responsibility, and repented. Instead, a grudge was nursed and revenge was sought.

Resisting Revenge

Revenge is an angry response to being treated in wrong ways, but it is not a godly response. Scripture tells us that revenge is the Lord's and we need to leave it to him.

Revenge doesn't solve anything anyway. It only ups the ante for more hatred and anger, which negatively impacts the body, only serving to hurt the person seeking revenge. If you find yourself wanting revenge, these biblical prescriptions may help curb that urge.

1. *Be slow to speak and to become angry.* "My dear brothers and sisters, take note of this: Everyone should be quick to listen, slow to speak and slow to become angry" (James 1:19).
2. *Examine your heart.* What do you desire? "A quick-tempered person does foolish things, and the one who devises evil schemes is hated" (Prov. 14:17).
3. *Find the lesson in the anger.* Is there something that needs to be corrected, changed, or dealt with better? Look for the lesson. "Tremble and do not sin; when you are on your beds, search your hearts and be silent" (Ps. 4:4).
4. *Observe your feelings.* Acknowledge the feeling and then let it go. Practice calming techniques. "Better a patient person than a warrior, one with self-control than one who takes a city" (Prov. 16:32).
5. *Don't allow your anger to escalate.* "A hot-tempered person must pay the penalty; rescue them, and you will have to do it again" (Prov. 19:19).
6. *Regroup.* "Fools give full vent to their rage, but the wise bring calm in the end" (Prov. 29:11).
7. *Have a big-picture perspective.* Is your anger worth the relationship? Is it more important to be right than to be merciful? "But now you must also rid yourselves of all such things as these: anger, rage, malice, slander, and filthy language from your lips" (Col. 3:8).

8. *Surround yourself with people who exercise self-control.* "Do not make friends with a hot-tempered person, do not associate with one easily angered" (Prov. 22:24).

Working with Anger in Positive Ways

Russ and Jenna were at it again. Russ was driving like a maniac through busy traffic. Jenna reacted to his driving with anger. But Jenna realized that when she does react with anger, the problem escalates. It usually goes like this.

"Hey, slow down. You're driving way too fast!"

"I know how to drive and don't need to be told what to do. When was the last time I got a ticket?"

"Really? Stop being a jerk and slow down! You always think you're right."

This demanding and yelling approach usually escalated to an angry pitch. When that happened, Russ would become overwhelmed. So Jenna decided to take another, more positive approach to the problem.

"Hey, slow down. You're driving way too fast!"

"I know how to drive and don't need to be told what to do. When was the last time I got a ticket?"

"That's not the point! I don't want to die today. I need a manicure and clean underwear!"

The couple laughed and the tension disappeared. Russ slowed down a little and Jenna relaxed. One person knew how to deescalate conflict when it came to a boiling point. Just when Russ was starting to feel annoyed and angry, Jenna cracked a joke. Humor was a way of repairing the moment. Jenna's humor lowered the heat, making them both laugh and relax.

When one person makes a positive effort to reduce stress in the other, anger settles down. This happens several ways between healthy people.

Here are a few of those ways:

1. *Humor breaks the tension.* Jenna understood this way of keeping anger at bay. She confronted the problem but did it in a way that broke tension.

2. *Ask yourself if there is any truth to what the other person is saying.* It's easy to go on the defensive when confronted. But instead of reacting with anger, pause and ask if there is any truth to what the person is saying.

3. *Express some affection or a word of caring during an argument.* Adding a positive in the middle of a problem softens the blow.

4. *Use a momentary distraction to lower tension.* You can say something like, "Your hair sure looks good today." Or "I'm thinking about how much I love you."

5. *Agree to one point of positive change.* If you stay angry, you can't think. So slow down that anger emotion and think about a change you could make that would help the situation.

6. *Be empathetic.* Empathy keeps anger levels down. If you can see the other person's perspective, you will better understand the person and their motivation.

7. *Change your negative thought to a positive one that makes you feel valuable.* If you really struggle with angry thoughts that come from feeling inadequate or worthless, think about a time you were successful or did something positive. Better yet, think about how God values you.

8. *Tolerate distress and tension, knowing it won't last forever.* This is part of maturing.

9. *Focus on your response as a choice.* You can harm or help.

10. *Check your physical and mental states.* If you are tired, sick, hungry, anxious, overwhelmed, etc., you are more likely to respond poorly. Wait until you feel better to address an important issue.

11. *Make improving the moment your goal.* This will help you avoid negative behavior like blaming.

So let's put it all together with Nathan and Mary.

Nathan and Mary had been in my office many times. Their arguing often escalated to anger, and Nathan would have a hard time calming down. The help I gave Nathan may help you. It is a way to approach the anger problem that kept surfacing in his relationship with Mary.

1. *Nathan needs to admit that his anger is out of control.* While anger is a normal emotion and not a sin, anger expression can be sinful. When Nathan cursed, yelled, screamed at, and disrespected Mary, this was a problem.

2. *Nathan needs to realize that venting his anger won't make him feel better.* We already know that venting leads to more aggression. Nathan has to revisit this belief and accept that there is no evidence to support this strategy.

3. *Nathan needs to get at the root of his anger.* Nathan is triggered by issues from his past. He is asked to keep an anger log to see what triggers his explosions. Below the surface, Nathan feels hurt and vulnerable, a position that makes him uncomfortable. Anger makes him feel powerful. He didn't feel powerful as a child. But Nathan is an adult and not a victim of his past. He can react differently. His wife is not his critical mother! He targets his hot buttons so he can prepare a different response.

4. *Nathan practices ways to calm down and commits to using them.* We rehearse several strategies—deep breathing, taking a time-out, counting to ten, creating a distraction, etc. Nathan practices deep muscle relaxation at night as a way to calm down his body.

5. *Nathan studies the biblical passages on anger*—be slow to vent, deal with anger when it comes up, no name-calling, get to the source, etc. He prays and stays close to God, knowing that a fruit of the Spirit is self-control.

6. *Nathan is able to stay calm during the next argument* since he knows his triggers, has worked through issues of his past, and is armed with new ways to calm himself.

7. *The two people discuss what went right.* Nathan identified his anger triggers, employed the calming strategy, stuck to the guidelines, and waited to talk until he was calm.

Nathan had to unlearn his immediate response to anger. The reason he was successful was because he committed to improving his relationships. He was willing to work on issues from his past that were affecting his present. With no good role models on how to deal with anger, Nathan developed his own strategies for calming down. This included a cue from his wife. With practice, Nathan's anger response is no longer a problem.

Conflict, whether great or small, brings tension and struggle. Injustice and unfair treatment characterize a fallen world that is yet to be redeemed. But staying angry over what you can't change blocks your personal healing. Approaching what you can change with a hostile or defensive attitude doesn't lead to problem solving or relationship satisfaction. Revenge doesn't work.

There will be a day when every conflict will end with justice. God will judge those who have hurt us. Offenses will be righted. Until then, we have to do our best to deal with anger and not let it deal us a negative hand.

For now, do your part. Express anger in a way that pleases God and doesn't hurt you or other people. When you do, anger will not rule your life.

13

Forgiveness

Forgiveness does not change the past, but it does enlarge the future.

Paul Boese

It was the holidays, and my husband and I were having a disagreement over whose Christmas party to attend. Unfortunately, both parties were on the same date and at the same time. He was working at a television network, and I was on the faculty of a medical school. Both of us felt it important to have the other at our party. So we began a discussion over the conflict. At times, we got loud but never disrespectful. We were both passionate about our arguments.

My mother-in-law was visiting and is uncomfortable with conflict. Conflict triggers issues from her past. In the middle of us trying to resolve our dilemma, my mother-in-law stepped between us and quoted Matthew 5:9, "Blessed are the peacemakers, for they shall be called the children of God."

She physically stood between us and wouldn't let us talk. Both of us were startled. First of all, we were not upset with each other. We were disagreeing and attempting to come to a solution to our problem. Both of us were giving our sides of the argument. And the Scripture that was quoted was used out of context. Matthew 5:9 is a reference to our peace with God as his children and to our wholeness and well-being as we walk with God. We weren't warring parties needing reconciliation. We were simply confronting a problem.

The word *peace* comes from the Greek word *eireinel*, meaning a mental attitude of tranquility based on one's relationship with Christ. It is the peace we have knowing God is with us and will be with us through difficult times. Peace opposes worry and is a fruit of the Spirit.

In terms of relationships, we are not keeping the peace when we try to cover up or avoid problems. Think about the story of Absalom and his brother Amnon found in 2 Samuel 13. Absalom and Tamar were brother and sister from King David's wife Maacah. Amnon was David's firstborn son from another wife, Ahinoam. Amnon became lovesick for Tamar, yet could not have her because she was his half sister and a virgin waiting for marriage. But Amnon plotted to get Tamar into his bed and eventually raped her.

When Absalom found out, he temporarily kept the peace by telling Tamar to deal with her shame and hide. When King David learned what happened, he was angry but did nothing, thus enabling his son the rapist. Absalom decided to avenge his sister by plotting against Amnon rather than confronting him head-on. There was no attempt to work through a family conflict. For two years, Absalom hid his anger and plotted his revenge. This temporary peace resulted in a life of shame for Tamar, the death of Amnon, and Absalom's alienation from his father, David.

Modern times are not that different. We try to temporarily keep the peace. We may try to fix the problem so the person who created it doesn't feel the consequences immediately. This is called enabling. Enabling involves our attempts to help people by repeatedly bailing them out, giving them one more chance, ignoring the problem, joining them in the same behaviors (avoiding), accepting excuses, avoiding problems, doing for them what they should do for themselves, removing the natural consequences, rescuing them, or trying to control them or their problems. Enabling prevents people from learning to work through conflict.

Enabling is about not rocking the boat. It is a temporary measure that reduces conflict in the moment but brings negative consequences in the long run. This was the case with Anthony. His parents would not confront his drug use because of the push back they got from him. In order to keep the peace, they bought Anthony's lies. They took his side whenever he got into trouble and blamed others for his problems. The family peace was seriously broken when Anthony ended up in jail. It took the legal system to confront Anthony's drug use. His parents then realized that keeping the peace temporarily was not a good idea when it involved enabling.

To truly keep the peace, one has to stay open to confronting problems. In the process, we allow people to figure out a solution before jumping in too quickly; we create appropriate boundaries and let people feel the consequences of their actions. We also listen to what others say and try not to speak for them or assume that they have the same point of view we do. We have to rock the boat, but not tip it!

One way to keep the peace is to address problems as soon as possible so they don't grow into issues of contention. It's when we sit on problems that resentment and anger build. And when we can't agree, keeping the peace may require bringing in a third party to help. A mediator can often help us get to a common goal or solution.

Keeping the peace does mean letting go of the need to be right during an argument. For example, is it really important to be "right" about how the toothpaste is squeezed or if the toilet paper should roll in or out? Sometimes, we keep the peace by compromising. We meet the person halfway and both give a little. But keeping the peace cannot proceed without forgiveness.

The Power of Forgiveness

Debbie's Story

It was the worst loss-of-life accident in the history of the state of Wyoming. Five days after 9-11 shook our nation, eight members of the University of Wyoming cross-country and track teams were traveling south of Laramie in an SUV and were hit head-on in a collision by a one-ton pickup truck driven by a fellow student. The accident had such impact that all the boys, except the driver, were thrown into a ditch one hundred yards away.

The driver, Clint Haskins, was a twenty-one-year-old senior at the University of Wyoming. Clint was attending the school on a rodeo scholarship and had been out partying that night. According to the *LA Times* report, it wasn't the first time Clint put away rounds of beer and whiskey and then got in his truck to drive. This fateful night in September he was on his way to see his girlfriend in Colorado. On an obscure winding road he veered into oncoming traffic and hit the Jeep carrying the boys. Clint has no memory of what happened when his truck plowed into the boys. There was no trial. He pleaded guilty and was given a fourteen-to-twenty-year sentence for eight counts of vehicular homicide and sent to a maximum security prison.

Debbie McLeland, mom to one of the boys, heard the knock on her door early that morning of the accident. A policeman delivered news no parent ever wants to hear. Her son's death hit her hard. She was angry and held on to that anger for several months.

But Debbie had a unique perspective. As the mom of three sons, she believed that Clint would wake up one day and realize what he had done. She didn't see Clint as an evil person but as a young man who made a terrible decision. He would have to live with what he did the rest of his life.

Debbie thought about revenge and the notion of an eye for an eye, but she knew that path would take her nowhere. Hatred, according to Debbie, is a big burden to carry. Debbie wanted justice, not revenge, and chose the road of forgiveness to deal with her loss.

Three years after the accident, Debbie traveled to the Wyoming State Penitentiary to meet Clint Haskins. Her response to meeting him surprised people. She hugged him and sincerely believed he was sorry. She decided the two of them could bring some good out of such tragedy.

What has happened since has been astounding. She and Clint have partnered against drunk driving. They have appeared on the same stage together, embracing each other and giving their message to not drink and drive. Debbie felt the two of them could have a real impact on others.

Yes, Debbie was angry that she lost her son. But her way of dealing with it was to forgive and move forward to reconcile with her son's killer. Not all the parents who lost sons were in agreement with what Debbie did. Some of the parents were angered by Debbie's response, feeling she had turned Clint into a celebrity. Others thought he should rot in his cell. Some felt offering forgiveness was being disloyal to their loved one. But Debbie felt that holding on to unforgiveness would only keep anger and bitterness alive in her heart. She desperately wanted to leave that place of pain and hurt and move forward.

According to Debbie, her response was motivated by what she believes about her son and her faith. She believes her son Morgan would want her to forgive. He understood forgiveness. And she wanted her faith to be less about rules and more about how she lives her life.

What Debbie may not know is that the part of her brain that is activated when she forgives is the anterior cingulate cortices, the part associated with empathy. The part associated with revenge comes from the same part of the brain that looks for something to eat when we are hungry. It is the desire to satisfy a craving. If you give in to it, you satisfy the craving in the short run.

While we may hunger for revenge, forgiveness is better for recovering and moving forward. It is restorative. In this case, forgiveness was truly divine and vengeance was left to God.[1]

I was in a workshop conducted by Christian psychiatrist Dr. Paul Meier at the World Conference of the American Association of Christian Counselors. As he lectured, he talked about the importance of forgiveness as a process that usually takes awhile. It's true. Even when we choose to forgive, our feelings take time to catch up to our mind.

Forgiveness, he reminded us, helps a person retain serotonin, a chemical involved in mood that the body naturally produces. Forgiveness helps people alleviate depression by naturally restoring serotonin, a mood-boosting neurotransmitter.

Only in recent years has the mental health community discovered the benefits of forgiveness. Forgiveness enhances health and relationships and even prevents disease.

Sheri's Story

Sheri grew up in a small town in Rhode Island. Nothing too exciting ever happened in that tiny town. One year, a country singer came through town on a tour bus and stopped at the local diner. People were crazy with excitement and talked about their celebrity moment for years.

In small towns, everyone knows everyone, or at least they think they do. Sheri's daddy worked at the local hardware store. He was a quiet man who didn't make trouble. Her mom bagged groceries at the only grocery store in town. Sheri, the oldest of three sisters, would occasionally help her mom at the store, but mostly, she watched her younger sisters.

In the summers, the three sisters spent most of their time outdoors. The warm summer sun felt good against their pale skin. The meadow near their house served as a natural playground. There, they could run, play tag, and make small sailboats sail on the creek.

Sheri was especially good at making beautiful bouquets with the wildflowers in the field. Mostly the girls laughed, made up stories, and dreamed of big adventures in the nearby city.

Inside the walls of their house, however, life was not so carefree. Sheri's dad had a drinking problem that folks never saw. After work, he would sit in front of the TV with some awful-smelling whiskey in his glass. That's when all hell broke loose. Some nights, he would be tired and fall asleep in the chair. But on those nights when he seemed particularly restless, Sheri and her sisters tried to stay out of his sight.

Sheri's youngest sister, Sarah, usually hid under her bed on Dad's restless nights. The sound of his footsteps entering her room practically made her heart stop. Sheri's middle sister, Annie, was too scrappy to hide. She was the most like Daddy. If Daddy came near her in his drunken state, she would punch him. She was tall and athletic and a physical match for him. Once, when he tried to grab her, she bit him on the arm. And Mom, well, she was nowhere to be found on the nights Daddy got mean. She disappeared.

Sometimes Daddy would find Sarah. When that happened, Sheri would push her 5'4" frame between Daddy and Sarah and say, "Take me. You've got me. Leave her alone." An evil grin would cross Daddy's face, and the nightmare would begin. For years, Sheri was the target of her father's rage and sexual abuse.

One weekend, Sheri's friends convinced her to get out of the house and go with them to the nearby military base to meet some men. During that trip, she met Bill, a quiet, gentle man with a kind smile. Even though Sheri had put on weight as a way of coping with the constant abuse, Bill seemed interested in her and spent the evening getting to know her.

For months, Sheri secretly dated Bill. Six months into the relationship, Bill asked Sheri to marry him, but Sheri was worried about her sister Sarah. Annie could take care of herself and had already moved out.

She had to tell Bill what was going on inside her home, but she was afraid Bill might call off the engagement when he found out. Daddy always told her that she was damaged goods and no man would want her, especially knowing what a "tramp" she was.

When Bill listened to the horror of what Sheri's dad did to her, he was so angry and said he wanted to kill him. Of course, he reassured Sheri that he would never do such a thing. But this had to stop. Sheri knew it was time to face her dad. Bill would help her and be by her side.

Sheri found a counselor to help with the confrontation. The counselor made it clear that there was no guarantee that her dad would admit to his actions or take responsibility. In fact, his anger could intensify. She needed a plan to handle the confrontation, and together they made a plan for Sheri's safety and prepared her heart. Sheri hoped for the best but prepared for the worst.

Just as the counselor predicted, the confrontation was a nightmare. Sheri's father called her horrific names, denied any wrongdoing, and accused her of coming on to him. Then he threatened to come after her if she told this lie to anyone. But Sheri did not back down. Calmly, with resolve, she looked him in the eyes and said, "Do what you have to do because I am not backing down this time. I'm taking Sarah and you will never see us again."

Sheri's dad slammed the door so hard she thought it would fall off the hinges. Sarah fell in her arms sobbing and the two walked out of the house and never looked back.

Years later, Sheri was shopping at her local grocery store in a state far away from Rhode Island. As she was moving down the produce aisle, she looked up. Her father, much shorter than she remembered, was standing next to a display of fruit. She couldn't believe it. What was he doing here in this faraway place after all these years? Before she could move, he began to walk toward her. Her heart pounded, her knees went weak. She felt like fainting.

The closer he came, the more she could see how disheveled he looked. He had aged beyond his years. His once strong body had thinned, and he was moving with difficulty. "I know I have no right to talk to you," he said. "I never thought I would see you again. But I want to say I'm sorry. I've been looking for you this past year to tell you that I'm ready to talk to the police. You see, I met a woman after I left your mom and she introduced me to God. I know you won't believe me, but I've changed and want to make things right."

Sheri froze right there next to the vegetables. The confrontation she had with him long ago had almost ruined her life, and now he wanted forgiveness? The monster had declared he had changed, and she was supposed to believe it?

Stunned, she couldn't move or speak. She had spent a year in therapy dealing with the fallout of the sexual abuse and her father's denial. In one of the sessions, her therapist asked, "What would you do if you saw your dad again?"

Sheri had given this question much thought. She predicted she would be afraid of him and most likely want to hurt him for all the pain he caused her. The rage inside her was intense. But standing in front of him now, she almost felt sorry for him. He was broken, a man she had never seen before. Instead of anger, she felt pity.

Would she forgive him? After all he had done to her, no one would fault her if she walked away. He should suffer like she did. He should pay for what he had done and not be given any mercy. But even though Sheri had every right to walk away and condemn him for his actions, she couldn't.

Sheri understood too much about forgiveness. She had been working on this with the therapist and meditating on Mark 11:25: "And when you stand praying, if you hold anything against anyone, forgive them, so that your Father in heaven may forgive you your sins." In Matthew 6:15 Jesus adds, "But if you do not forgive others their sins, your Father will not forgive your sins." These words were hard to swallow as she stood by her father.

She knew that she had to forgive him because God forgives her. This meant she really had to give up her right to resentment and judgment. She had to once and for all let go of wishing her dad harm and ask God to foster feelings of compassion toward this pitiful man. Sheri prayed silently, asking the Holy Spirit to work in her.

Then she burst into tears. "Yes, I forgive you. I had to long ago even though I never thought I would hear you repent. If I didn't choose to forgive, I would still live in the prison you built for me. And I wanted to be free. I had to release you so I could move on. You are in God's hands in terms of your actions toward me. He will be your final judge."

Sobbing, Sheri turned away and walked out of the store. A month later, she learned that her father had turned himself in and was attending a program for sexual abusers as part of his prison sentence. The therapist asked if she would attend a family session. Her sisters would be there, along with her mother.

Everything in Sheri wanted to say no. The lost years, the deep pain. Was any type of repair even possible? But she agreed to go.

And while she was not able to trust her dad or have a close relationship with him, she was able to confront the horror of her childhood and move on. Her road to healing was not easy, and some of her friends suggested she seek revenge or never speak to her father again. But Sheri wanted emotional freedom and found it through her choice to forgive.

Hopefully, her story will encourage you. Forgiveness brings healing. It releases you from the power of resentment and bitterness.

Riley Cooper and Michael Vick's Story

We live in a time when people are ultrasensitive to offenses, maybe rightfully so. But the way an offense is handled can either lead to more anger and unforgiveness or healing. This is a true story from the National Football League involving racial offense, a cultural hot button we've already discussed.

A white football player from the Philadelphia Eagles, Riley Cooper, attended a Kenny Chesney concert in July 2013 with some friends. During a Chesney song, Cooper was pulled onstage to perform "Boys of Fall" with the singer and band. Cooper was admittedly drinking and directed a racial slur to an African-American security guard at the concert. It was all captured on video.

Once the media saw the incident, he was taken to task. He was fined by the Philadelphia Eagles and issued an apology saying he was both ashamed and disgusted by his actions. His teammates tried to deal with the racial slur in a way that did not invite grudges and offense.

Racial slurs, bullying, and any unkind remarks are never okay. We have to do better at examining the prejudice and discrimination we hold in our hearts toward those who are different from us. In fact, the Bible tells us that every careless word will be judged one day. Ouch!

I am not condoning what Cooper did. Please hear this. But last time I looked, we are all flawed. In fact, we are sinners, falling very short of the glory of God. We make mistakes. Sometimes we say terrible things we later regret. Our hearts are exposed for the darkness we hide.

What if we were videoed 24/7 at home, on the job, etc.? How would our lives appear to others scrutinizing our tapes? This doesn't excuse what Cooper said, but it informs our response and speaks to what happened next.

During the NFL incident, Michael Vick, an African-American quarterback for the Eagles, handled the situation with grace. Vick, who had been the target of unrelenting media scrutiny for his previous mistakes involving a dog-fighting scandal, learned something from his past. He learned the importance of grace and forgiveness.

Vick said of his teammate, Cooper, "Riley is still my teammate. And he just stood in front of us as a man and apologized for what he said. And somewhere deep down, you have to find some level of respect for that. Riley wished he never said it."

Vick went on to say, "As a team we understood because we all make mistakes in life and we all do and say things that maybe we do mean and maybe we don't mean. But as a teammate, I forgave him. We understand the magnitude of the situation. We understand a lot of people may be hurt and offended, but I know Riley Cooper. I know him as a man. I've been with him for the last three years, and I know what type of person he is. That's what makes it easy, and at the same time, hard to understand. But easy to forgive him."[2]

Forgiveness didn't mean that Vick agreed with what Cooper did or minimized the impact of his words. Offering forgiveness meant Vick recognized the severity of the breach. To forgive someone means you acknowledge the wrong. In no way does forgiveness mean you condone what someone does.

Michael Vick's brother, Marcus Vick, had a different response and embarked on a Twitter tirade, calling Riley all kinds of expletives and calling for a bounty on Cooper's head. His tweets—angry and hateful—were the opposite of his brother's.

Forgiveness goes against our natural bent toward revenge. Romans 12:19–21 addresses this: "Do not take revenge, my dear friends, but leave room for God's wrath, for it is written: 'It is mine to avenge; I will repay,' says the Lord. On the contrary: 'If your enemy is hungry, feed him; if he is thirsty, give him something to drink. In doing this, you will heap burning coals on his head.' Do not be overcome by evil, but overcome evil with good."

First Peter 2:22–23 adds, "'He [Jesus] committed no sin and no deceit was found in his mouth.' When they hurled their insults at him, he did not retaliate; when he suffered, he made no threats. Instead, he entrusted himself to him who judges justly." The implication is that we are to leave judgment and retaliation to God. This doesn't mean that people won't pay for their crimes or be confronted on their behavior. It means that in our hearts, we must be careful to not sit as judge, knowing that God will judge every person one day.

Both Vick brothers responded to the same conflict. One brother chose empathy and forgiveness and tried to calm down the situation. The other brother returned the injustice. We control how we respond.

Grace versus the Law

Like the Vick brothers, two characters in Victor Hugo's *Les Misérables* also faced a choice regarding grace or the law. Javert, the unrelenting officer who would not rest until he brought Valjean, the former convict, to justice, had the tables turned on him. Valjean had a chance to kill Javert when he was caught on the wrong side of enemy lines. Javert deserved no favors from Valjean, the target of his obsession for years.

Valjean made a choice to spare Javert's life. He refused to retaliate and showed mercy, allowing Javert to escape. But grace was not in the heart of Javert. He continued to hunt Valjean in order to make him pay for his crime, despite Valjean's change for the good.

In a desperate scene, Javert's bitterness and unforgiveness led to his suicide. He could not grasp the power of love or the forgiveness of God. The story is a powerful reminder of the two possible paths—grace versus law; forgiveness versus bitterness.

Forgiveness is a choice. Valjean accepted responsibility for his crimes and submitted himself to the law. He was freed by the power of love and forgiveness. Forgiveness frees us, emotionally, physically, and spiritually.

Forgiveness is not about what people deserve. Valjean did not deserve another chance, but he got one. None of us deserves forgiveness, yet God gives it to us. We only have to look to the most powerful example of Christ and his final moments on the cross. Wrongly accused, without sin, abused, naked, and thirsty, he took all the undeserved punishment. Hanging on the tree, close to death, Jesus says, "Father, forgive them, for they do not know what they are doing" (Luke 23:34).

Forgiveness is your choice. It frees you from bitterness. It lowers your heart rate and blood pressure and relieves stress. Forgiveness jump-starts the process of reconciliation.

The person who nurses a grudge suffers spiritually, emotionally, and physically. Like in Javert's case, grudges preoccupy our thinking to the point that we can't enjoy the present. We are too busy nursing the offense and looking for ways to retaliate.

You may be feeling this now. Something unfair may have happened to you. It happens to all of us, me included.

I was treated unfairly by someone well known in the Christian community. There was no apology and no indication that the offense would ever be acknowledged. Confronting the offense meant I would have to go after the person legally. My lawyers said do it. I wanted to right the wrong.

My anger was mixed with disbelief. I saw what looked like God blessing this person. I was hurt that someone willingly chose not to do the right thing because he was afraid and would not stand up for his conviction of what was right. The more I thought and talked about the situation, the angrier I became. Thinking about an angry situation over and over does not help. In fact, Dr. Everett Worthington, a leading researcher on forgiveness at Virginia Commonwealth University, says this about continuing to think about the offense: "Chronic unforgiveness causes stress. Every time people think of their transgressor, their body responds. Forgiving cuts your health risk and strengthens the immune system."[3] I didn't want my physical health affected. I didn't want to give the person that kind of power.

I had to deal with the anger. I know, life isn't fair, people do not always act the way they are supposed to. Intellectually, I understand why someone would do the wrong thing. However, my feelings had to catch up with my head.

So, I chose to forgive the person and refused to hang on to the offense. As I released the person with forgiveness, I asked God to heal the hurt I felt. I meditated on 1 Peter 2:22–23—Jesus left his case in the hands of God. That is a good place to leave the offense—in the hands of God.

And like Peter, I found myself asking how many times do I have to forgive? Our Lord's response? "I tell you, not seven times, but seventy-seven times" (Matt. 18:21–22). Again, I don't like forgiving repeat and unrepentant offenders, but I knew I had to or I would pay the price.

The process of letting go isn't easy when the offense impacts your life in a major way. Some things are harder to forgive than others. Dr. Worthington, whom I quoted earlier, knows a thing or two about forgiveness. He had to apply everything he studied and researched on the topic to his personal life. At 7:00 a.m., New Year's Day, 1996, he received a frantic call from his brother telling him that their seventy-six-year-old mother had been brutally beaten, sexually abused, and then murdered.

Worthington was so angry, he wanted to go after the killer with a baseball bat and beat him to death. The moment Worthington decided to forgive his mother's killer, he said, "I saw myself looking at the baseball bat. I thought to myself, 'Whose heart is darker—mine or his?' That was the moment when I forgave him. It changed my whole life."[4]

When people do things that are horrible and unfair, we choose a path. Forgiveness and refusal to nurse a grudge will eventually end in healing. God is the only judge and jury on the state of our hearts. Our job is to forgive and let God do the rest.

Forgiving Ourselves

Sometimes, we can be our own worst enemy and need to forgive ourselves. When we have been the one who has committed the injustice or has hurt someone else, forgiving ourselves is often blocked by the shame we feel. We beat ourselves up.

We block the healing process by not accepting God's grace. His sacrifice takes care of our sins and mistakes, wipes them clean, and allows us to do a spiritual do over. When we accept what he has already done for us, we can live in freedom.

To forgive yourself means to acknowledge your mistakes or sin, confess, make amends where and when possible, and then let go of the guilt. You can't change what has happened, but you can accept God's offer to live in freedom.

14

We Can Work It Out

Be strong, and let your heart take courage, all you who hope in the Lord.

Psalm 31:24

It was a typical Sunday night. The kids were crying, Rick was hesitant to leave, and JoAnne stood in the doorway feeling uncomfortable. A weekend with Dad always ended in tears. The children hated this all-too-familiar drill.

Rick and JoAnne had been married for fifteen years when they decided to call it quits. They knew it would be hard on their young children but never anticipated the emotional intensity regularly encountered. From the kids' perspective, Mom and Dad needed to work out their problems and get back together.

Watching how painful separation was for their children every weekend, Rick and JoAnne wondered if they had acted prematurely. They had never tried marital counseling or talked to their pastor. They were gridlocked on so many issues that they just gave up trying and decided to call it quits. Both wanted a break from the unhappy marriage.

The marriage had never quite gelled. Neither was good at accommodating the other. Rick wanted more time with his friends, and JoAnne wanted him home more. Of course, there were other differences and areas of conflict—failing to follow through on promises, refusing to help around the house, unresolved issues over child care . . . the list seemed endless.

When they decided to separate, they both said they were sorry the marriage didn't work. Apologies were accepted, but there were no attempts at reconciliation. Neither was interested in taking an honest look at the issues in the marriage. Escape seemed to be a better route. It was less painful, so they thought.

Both Rick and JoAnne were raised in the church and knew that reconciliation is the heart of God. They understood that God's desire was that they be reconciled to him first, and then reconciled to each other (see Matt. 5:24). They just tried not to think about that, given the emotional pain of the relationship.

JoAnne admitted that she was the one who sparked the separation with her flirting online. She became emotionally attached to a former co-worker. When Rick confronted her, she refused to end the relationship, feeling the co-worker was more attentive than Rick. Rick refused to listen to her.

Months into the separation, JoAnne ended the emotional affair and apologized to Rick for turning away from him. She knew her behavior was wrong. Rick accepted the apology but wasn't interested in reconciling the marriage. The sting of JoAnne's rejection and betrayal hurt too much. And there were so many other issues.

Now, months later, Rick was willing to consider reconciliation. The impact the separation was having on the kids was hard to watch—crying, begging, and pleading for Mom and Dad to be together. But Rick knew if he and JoAnne gave it a try, they would have to address the issues that had been ignored for years. Would the two of them be able to do this? And would they be able to resurrect the loving feelings they once had for each other?

The couple decided to see a marriage therapist, feeling their previous efforts to do nothing got them nowhere. Both were surprised by the push back they received from their families. Rick's family told him not to try. They were angry with JoAnne and called her self-centered and stubborn. In their minds, an apology wasn't enough. They didn't trust her.

But Rick was thinking about his covenant with JoAnne. Yes, she breached his trust, but to be fair, he also ignored her needs. He hadn't been emotionally available to her. And because JoAnne realized that she handled his lack of attention poorly, Rick had hope. She was taking responsibility for her part of the problems. It was time for him to do the same.

JoAnne's family wanted her to move on as well. They were angry with Rick for leaving his family so easily. In their minds, he wasn't worth keeping. They sided with JoAnne and justified her looking outside the marriage for emotional support. JoAnne knew better.

Rick and JoAnne decided to tune out the voices around them and listen to their hearts. They also started praying together, asking for wisdom and direction.

When Rick and JoAnne began to work with a therapist, they learned to talk to each other without shouting. JoAnne's real desire was to be closer to Rick and have a deep intimacy. Rick took responsibility for escaping the issues of his marriage by hanging out with his guy friends. He admitted he didn't know how to handle JoAnne's emotions or be close to her. It was time for him to mature and be a husband.

Because the two were able to approach reconciliation with willingness and accept responsibility for their parts of the problem, the therapy worked. Neither wanted a future separated from their children. Both wanted a deeper intimacy.

A positive sign in the therapy was that both recalled their dating relationship as a happy time and were interested in restoring their feelings of love. Maybe having children and ignoring the marital friendship played into their growing apart.

JoAnne also realized she had to be accountable to Rick about her online behavior. Even though she no longer felt a need to look for emotional support from old friends and flames, she did need to rebuild trust by staying off-line. It was important to Rick. Her words of apology had to be backed up by a change in behavior. Rick needed to see that she meant what she said.

Both also realized that the way they dealt with their differences needed work. The children were upset by the way they fought. Rick and JoAnne didn't like the people they became during their fights. So JoAnne promised to start a conflict discussion in a softer way, with no attacking or blaming. Rick promised to stay in the discussion and only take a time-out when he felt overwhelmed. The two worked with the therapist to listen better and be less reactive.

Rick and JoAnne also joined a Sunday school class in their church. They wanted to be spiritually encouraged in their marriage. The class was a marriage mentoring class in which older, happy couples shared their stories of success with younger couples. The older couples talked about "rough spots" in their marriages and how they learned to grow during those times. Rather than throwing in the towel, they committed to working through problems. Some didn't need outside help. Others enlisted a therapist or pastor.

Reconciliation for Rick and JoAnne took over a year. They worked very hard at restoring their marital friendship and expressing fondness for each other. They revisited their dreams and expectations that once drew them together. Their focus was on what they could create together to get back on track. They worked through their differences and resolved a number of conflict issues. They beat the odds.

According to US statistics, only 13 percent of couples reunite after separation. The rest, almost 87 percent, go on to divorce.[1] But Rick and JoAnne didn't care about the odds. They cared about repairing the damage to a failing relationship and building a future with their children.

Not all relationships have happy endings. When active addiction, untreated serious mental illness, abuse, or violence is in play, reconciliation is unsafe and unwise. Denial of serious problems that can hurt others keeps a person stuck and not able to move forward. Most times, professional help is needed, but the person has to want to change for reconciliation to take place. Intent has to be followed by action and true repentance.

The decision to reconcile depends on a softened heart, a willingness to change, and an acceptance of responsibility. How willing are you to realistically look at issues and decide to tackle them no matter how long-standing and painful they are? To reconcile, you also have to have a willing partner who agrees to patiently work it all out with you. Wounds that run deep take courage to touch, and the decision to reconcile is one that moves beyond forgiveness. Forgiveness is a necessary part of the process, but it is only a first step in a much longer process.

Can this be done? Yes, as I know nothing is impossible with God. For God to work, however, both people must cooperate and be committed to the process. God gave us a will and does not force us to do what we don't want to do.

The Decision to Try Again

The pain of a broken relationship is often difficult to heal. Years of hurt and resentment can feel too big to tackle. And the idea of embracing emotional pain without being able to control the other person means an uncertain outcome.

Reconciliation efforts are usually made because we still have feelings for the person and believe things could change. Yet, pride can stop us from pursuing reconciliation. Reconciliation is blocked when we don't admit wrongdoing and continue to blame others for our problems. The longer we wait, the more entrenched and estranged we become. We then begin to organize our lives without the people we once loved.

However, if we admit our faults, accept responsibility, and make every effort to repair the damage done, hope remains. Reconciliation is possible in even the most difficult of relationships. Brenda and her dad are proof.

After fifteen years of marriage, Jerry announced to his family on Christmas Eve that he was leaving. He had met another woman and was moving out of the area to be with her. At the time, Brenda was only a teenager and became physically ill from the news. All she remembers about that night is running to her room crying. Her dad didn't follow her or try to comfort her. He simply walked out the door.

Brenda's mom went into a deep depression. Blindsided by the news, she spent Christmas Day in bed. Brenda sat alone by the tree, frightened by the uncertainty of it all. She couldn't catch her breath and felt like she was suffocating. The house was still and eerily quiet. How could he leave so abruptly? That question would plague her for years. And how could he leave her, his only daughter?

Brenda's mom became emotionally paralyzed. She sank deeper and deeper into the depression and rarely spoke. She refused to see anyone for help and spent hours in her bedroom.

Brenda tried to cope by staying at school as long as possible. She told no one what happened over the Christmas break. She desperately missed her dad, and her mother's isolation frightened her. She began to think that there must be something terribly wrong with her that her dad would abandon her in the way he had. She must not be worth much if she could be left so easily.

Brenda felt that she needed to punish herself for not being good enough to make her dad stay. In her bedroom at night, she would take a small pocketknife and slowly cut on her arms and inner thighs. Watching the blood drip gave her a slight high and made her temporarily forget about her dad. She could see the blood and watch it run down her arm. The pain would numb her into an emotional state of escape. Finally, a little relief.

Brenda had found a way to cope with the hurt she felt each night. But the scars on her arms were becoming more noticeable. The weather was getting warmer, and she had to wear long sleeves to cover the marks. No one noticed because no one in Brenda's life was paying attention to her emotional state.

As soon as Brenda graduated from high school, she left home. Her mom remained depressed and was now on public assistance and barely functioning. Clearly, Brenda was on her own. She could depend on no one. A fresh start might help, so she moved to a nearby city. She got a job and a small apartment and continued to cut on her arms before she went to sleep each night.

One day at work, a co-worker noticed the marks on her arms. "It's probably none of my business, but I saw your arm. I know what that is. My sister used to do that. You need help." Brenda snapped, "Yeah, well, what I do on my own time is my business. Mind your own." But Brenda knew her co-worker was right. The cutting wasn't giving her the relief it once had. Her arms were getting scarred and she was becoming more depressed.

Another co-worker invited her to join friends at a bar after work. Brenda thought, *Why not? I can probably drink my loneliness away with these people.* She agreed to meet the group. By the time she got to the bar, her friends were well on their way to partying, and Brenda joined in. But sitting way across the room was a man who looked strangely familiar. She drank more but couldn't stop looking at this man. He was sitting alone.

The alcohol loosened her defenses enough for her to walk in his direction. As she moved around the tables, she got a closer look. Panic seized her. Her heart beat rapidly, her breathing became short, and she felt like she was going to be sick. Could that man be her father?

What should she do? Paralyzed, she simply stared. For years, she'd lived without hearing or seeing her father and tried not to look back. Emboldened by the alcohol, she decided to approach him and demand to know what happened. After all, he ruined the family and left her to fend for herself.

"Dad?" He didn't move or look at her. "Dad, is that you?" He stared at his drink. Brenda got louder. "Hey, I asked you a question." Silence. "It must be you. The dad I know is a coward and runs from people." He slowly turned his head toward her. It was him, an older and more frail version of her father.

"It's me. Brenda, I know who you are."

Brenda fell into the chair. She didn't know what to say or do. Tears were running down her cheeks. He was silent. "All I want to know, all I ever wanted to know, is why you left so suddenly and never came back for me."

"I don't have a good answer. How is your mother?"

"She's seriously depressed and has been for years. She's like a prisoner in the house. She won't talk to people or go out. It started that Christmas Eve when you left and it hasn't stopped. She's never recovered. I was completely alone."

"I'm so sorry, Brenda. I'm a bad person. I couldn't deal with life. I thought running away from everything and starting over would help. It didn't. The woman I left with cheated on me two weeks after we left town. She left me. I was too embarrassed to tell anyone, so I stayed away. I know that isn't a good reason for why I never contacted you. Truth is, I am a coward. I gave up everything and was duped. It's humiliating, and your mom and you deserved better."

"And you cutting us out of your life for good was the way to give us a better life? Did you ever think of how we were doing with that? Did you ever think we might be falling apart too? For years, I made up stories. Maybe my dad was kidnapped and couldn't come to me, maybe he moved out of the country or was working undercover. Whatever. And now you tell me this was all because *you* were humiliated? Really? This is the best you can do?"

Brenda jumped up from the table and ran out of the bar. Sobbing outside, she couldn't believe what she had just heard. What kind of man walked away from his family and made no effort to contact them or check on them? This was worse than she imagined. He offered no excuse but his weak character. Anger welled up through the tears. She wasn't enough for her own father to want her. The urge to cut was growing stronger. She needed to find a bathroom. But suddenly, a hand pressed into her shoulder.

"Where are you going? Okay, I don't know what just happened back there, but it was intense. Who was that guy and why are you running away? Come on, Brenda, let me take you home. You are not okay." Her friend guided her back to her car. "Look, I'm not trying to pry, but you need help. You can't live like this and cut on yourself for whatever reasons you do that. I'm spending the night, and in the morning, we are getting you help."

Brenda was too emotionally exhausted to fight. She conceded to the ride and allowed her friend to spend the night. In the morning, the friend called a local clinic and helped Brenda make an appointment. Brenda agreed. Someone was finally taking an interest in helping her. She didn't want to end up like her mom and realized she was heading in that direction. Maybe a counselor could help.

The counselor did help. She explained that the cutting was a coping strategy Brenda used to escape the pain. To stop, she would have to confront the wounds of her past. Brenda was ready. Seeing her dad brought it all to a head.

As she worked through the therapy and focused on her dad's leaving, the therapist asked if she was ready to forgive her father.

"Shouldn't he be the one to ask me for forgiveness? I was completely innocent. Did nothing. He left me."

"You are absolutely right. Did he ask you for forgiveness?"

"No, but he should have. He should have manned up and owned what he did. Instead he made stupid excuses. It was pitiful."

"So now what do you do with that? How do you move forward if you refuse to forgive him? You are giving him power in your life. Until you grieve this loss and choose to forgive, cutting and depression are likely to revisit you. Is this what you want?"

"Of course I don't want that, or I wouldn't be here. But there's got to be another way. If I forgive him, it's all on me again. I do the work. He does nothing. That just isn't fair."

"If you don't forgive him, you pay the price. You stay stuck and he continues to ruin your life. Is that fair? You're starting to take back your life. Forgiveness moves you forward. It's your choice, and I'll help you move through the feelings."

Brenda left the therapist's office feeling mad, hurt, sad, and anxious. But the more she thought about it, the more she felt the need to begin the forgiveness process. She didn't want to live her life being bitter and alone. Her mom made that choice, and it was debilitating.

For months, Brenda and the therapist worked on the issues around the abandonment. As she moved through the loss and decided to forgive, the therapist asked her what would be different if she saw her dad again.

"Well, the biggest difference is I wouldn't be so shell-shocked. But I don't know what I would say. He didn't ask for forgiveness."

"What if you gave it to him anyway? What if he wanted to try and build something with you now?"

"It's a little late for that. He had his chance."

"So you don't believe in second chances?"

"Well, of course I do. But not with my dad. He's not even asking for one."

"What if I contacted him and asked him to come to a session with us? And what if he agreed? Would you be willing to do this?"

"You want me to go after him when he never came after me? Why would I do that and risk the chance that he would reject me again?"

"So like your dad, you would prefer to live with the possible humiliation than try?"

Ouch. That felt unfair. But it was true. The only excuse Brenda's father gave was feeling too humiliated to try and reconcile. Was she doing the same? She hated this therapy stuff! Cutting was easier than facing all of this! But something deep inside knew better. If she didn't try, she would never know if she could make amends. And she missed having a dad in her life.

"Okay, I'm onboard. I know how to find him. I'll ask if he'll come and work on this. Most of me doesn't want to do this, but part of me knows I need to try."

Brenda did try. What looked like an impossible reconnection actually worked, but Brenda had to make the first move. For a while, that bothered her. She really wanted her dad to take the step to come after her. He didn't. He was a broken man, and the therapist put him in individual therapy before they started to work on the father-daughter relationship.

There was so much to confront involving years of pain. But Brenda will tell you that it was worth it in the end. Her message to anyone who will listen is this: Don't wait. Make the first move. Drop the tug-of-war rope and heal. Apologize for your part. Allow people to be responsible for their part. Forgive. Establish trust. Be patient and see what God can do.

Reconciliation is an opportunity to grow beyond the past and the pain, with the hope of creating something new. Brenda created something new with her dad. The years of loss could not be regained, but the present connection with her dad was a start. They could build something they never had before. For Brenda, that became enough. She chose to take what could be had, grieve what was lost, and build a new relationship. For the first time, she felt healing in her soul. Forgiveness unleashed the pain and reconciliation mended the loss.

Her mother chose to stay in that dark and depressed place. She held on to the isolation, hurt, and pain. She chose not to forgive and lived with bitterness. It didn't end well. When she died, Brenda was sad—such a waste of a once-vibrant life.

In Scripture, hope is referred to as a strong and confident expectation. The strength of that expectation comes because of what God can do in any situation. With hope, you expect without certainty and desire something better. Hope changes how we see ourselves and changes what we value. It affects our decisions to face conflict.

Hope opposes avoidance. It allows us to pursue a courageous life. More importantly, hope brings joy and peace into our lives. It protects us from becoming cynical or giving up.

I admit, I have lost hope with many of the broken relationships I have seen in therapy. But those who enlisted their faith in the healing process had an advantage others didn't have—they could be transformed by God's work in them. When they submitted themselves to God first, things began to change. Hope came alive. Couples that should never have been able to reconcile did because of Christ's work in them. Families that should never have been able to rebuild after broken trust, did. God can do anything with a broken but submitted vessel. Never give up hope in him.

Reconciliation One Day

The greatest story ever told involves a cosmic conflict between God in heaven and one of his creations, Lucifer. In the story, Lucifer became prideful and desired equality with God. His pride pitted him against the throne of God and positioned him as God's enemy.

A heavenly battle ensued, and Lucifer was defeated and forced to earth. Cast out of heaven, he became the leader of the force that opposes God. When the first humans, Adam and Eve, disobeyed God and sinned, they submitted themselves to this evil force. This "prince of this world" continues to oppose the people and things of God.

And while this story is yet to conclude, we know the ending. God prevails and the enemy is defeated. The conflict between good and evil gets resolved. God will ultimately deal with the fallen creature and serve justice. In the meantime, conflict between good and evil remains a battle here on earth. We feel the tension. We are still in the fight. Sometimes that fight is a real battle, and reconciliation is delayed. But hope does spring eternal. One day, all wrongs will be righted. Until then, we do what we can to make things right.

Final Thoughts

Navigating the Storms

The clouds begin to build. The sky changes and the air feels thick. A storm is brewing. Air pressure changes, and rain clouds darken. You can see the mighty buildup of the clouds. Two opposing fronts are about to collide. When they do, the instability creates a storm. Storms are beautiful to watch but frightening to weather.

When people clash over differences, as with a storm, instability is created. Knowing how to navigate during that rocky time is critical and has been the focus of this book. We began with the notion that life storms will come. Rather than avoid them, we navigate through them to the other side. How we do that is critical to our relationship health.

A visiting pastor once preached a sermon about airline pilots who are taught to navigate through storms. Storms can't be avoided when flying, so pilots are trained for the unstable weather they will encounter. What we learn from pilots can help us during times of interpersonal storms.

The first thing pilots are taught is to *stay calm*. They cannot afford to allow panic or fear to drive their decisions or reactions. When calm, they know what to do and can react from a position of confidence, not fear. Panic and fear are dangerous because they can create reactions not in the training. And when flying through a storm, following the training guidelines is of utmost importance.

I come from a long line of people who initially panic when a storm hits. We don't typically stay calm but react in ways that are not always helpful. This raises the intensity and brings fear to the table. It takes awhile for people to calm down. I married a man who does the opposite. He was raised on the mission field, and storms were a regular part of his life. There were no resources to help when trouble hit. As a result, he prayed. Prayer, as a first response to trouble, became a lifestyle pattern. It keeps panic and fear away. The key to staying calm is in our thinking. *God is in this. He is with me. I can get through this. He has my best in mind and uses all things for my good.* These thoughts are built on the promises of God and bring calm to the trouble.

Second, a pilot must *check their instruments*. They can't always go by feeling.

Pilots deal with a condition in which their feeling of up and down isn't always correct. Consequently, they have to rely on their instruments to give them correct information.

Many of us remember the sad day when John F. Kennedy Jr.'s small single-engine plane went into the heavy seas off Martha's Vineyard. The plane's radar track showed all the evidence of Kennedy's mind wobbling in the tortured confusion of a condition called vertigo. When Kennedy felt right-side up, the aircraft instruments were conveying a different message. They were telling him that his wings were steeply tilted to the right of level. The nose of the airplane was pointing way down and his airspeed was howling past the red line. Kennedy could not tell up from down or left from right because the airplane's path befuddles one's awareness of earth's gravity.

Going by feeling was deadly. When emotions drown out the flight instruments' reality, the pilot may be banking and diving at high speed but feeling, "No way! It can't be. I'm actually flying straight and level. I *feel* it is true."

But it is not true. Feelings cannot be trusted as the final authority of what the airplane is doing. The same is true for us. Feelings can't always be trusted to guide us properly. Better to check our instruments of prayer and the Word of God. When that person treats you unfairly, you feel anger and want revenge. Then you check God's Word. Forgiveness, not vengeance, registers on the instrument.

Third, when storms hit, you must *communicate with the tower*. The tower sees you on radar and has the big picture of where you are going. It sees the whole and the small dot you represent in that whole. Without the tower directing you, you can easily get lost in a storm.

Our tower is God. If we stay connected and communicate, God will direct us through the difficulty. Part of that communication includes crying out to God. I did a lot of that when my brother was killed. So did my dad. I've seen him cry twice in his ninety-three years—once when my mother, his wife of sixty-seven years, died and once when my brother was killed. From the ceiling of my basement bedroom, I heard him pounding his fists on the floor, crying out to God over the death of his oldest son. God heard it, handled it, and took my dad's burden as his own. Dad was communicating with the tower. While he didn't understand why his son had to die at such a young age, he trusted the tower to see the big picture.

And as I trusted the tower, God changed my trajectory from a career in law to one in psychology. He used this tragedy to comfort others who experience loss. He brought good out of sorrow. He sees the big picture and can be trusted to get us through the storm if we communicate with him.

Fourth, when pilots communicate with the tower, they must *comply with what they are told*. Because the tower has a better view of the weather and the aircraft, it guides you through the storm. The worst thing a pilot can do is go rogue.

God has given us a guide. It is his Word. In it, he tells us what to do so we don't go rogue. But like pilots, we have to decide to obey the instructions in order to be led out of the storm.

Finally, when the storm is too strong and could overcome the aircraft, pilots are taught to *climb higher* and get above the storm. As they move through the unstable air, the ride eventually levels off to a calmer, more peaceful place far above the storm clouds. They can see the storm below, but they rise above it.

Worship is our way to climb above the storm. As we immerse ourselves in God's presence, we fall into his arms to a place of rest and peace. We praise until the worship comes, worship until the glory comes, then sit at the feet of the One who loves us and washes his love over us. He takes us above the storm and brings peace to our anxious soul.

The clouds build. Storms hit. The air is turbulent and we are shaken.

We hear that dreaded phrase, "We need to talk . . ." Rather than feeling dread,

> Rejoice. Aim for restoration, comfort one another, agree with one another, live in peace; and the God of love and peace will be with you. (2 Cor. 13:11 ESV)

Take everything you've learned from this book and deal with conflict and differences. Don't allow bitterness and unforgiveness to take root. Keep the peace by addressing the hurt. Work through the pain. Don't escape it. Learn to approach conflict and differences with the confidence that you can work out relationship problems and live in peace.

In the book of Matthew, Jesus reminds his disciples that with God all things are possible. Will you trust the God of the possible? Will you make your relationships work?

> Now may the God of hope fill you with all joy and peace in believing, that you may abound in hope by the power of the Holy Spirit. (Rom. 15:13)

Notes

Chapter 1: Conflict

1. *Merriam-Webster.com*, http://www.merriam-webster.com/dictionary/conflict.

2. Janice M. Steil, *Marital Equality: Its Relationship to the Well-Being of Husbands and Wives* (Newbury Park Oaks, CA: Sage, 1997).

3. K. M. Quek and C. Knudson-Martin, "A Push Towards Equality: Process Among Dual-Income Couples in a Collectivist Culture," *Journal of Marriage and Family Therapy* 68 (2006): 56–69.

4. Lynn Price Cooke, "Doing Gender in Context: Household Bargaining and Risk of Divorce in Germany and the United States," *American Journal of Sociology* 112 (2006): 266–80.

5. Robert W. Beavers, *Successful Marriage: A Family Systems Approach to Couples Therapy* (New York: Norton, 1985).

Chapter 3: I'd Rather Not Talk

1. K. S. Birditt, E. Brown, T. L. Orbuch, and J. M. McIlvane, "Marital Conflict Behaviors and Implications for Divorce Over 16 Years," *Journal of Marriage and Family* 72, no. 5 (2010): 1188–204.

2. Ernest Harburg, Niko Kaciroti, Lillian Gleiberman, M. Anthony Schork, and Mara Julius, "Marital Pair Anger Coping Types May Act as an Entity to Affect Mortality: Preliminary Findings from a Prospective Study (Tecumseh, Michigan)," *Journal of Family Communication* 8 (2008): 44–61.

Chapter 4: Differences Make a Difference

1. "Blondes Take Longer Than Brunettes to Get Ready," *The Telegraph*, October 7, 2009, http://www.telegraph.co.uk/news/uknews/6268201/Blondes-take-longer-than-brunettes-to-get-ready.html.

2. Michael Lynn, "Determinants and Consequences of Female Attractiveness and Sexiness: Realistic Tests with Restaurant Waitresses," *Archives of Sexual Behavior* 38, no. 5 (2009): 737–45.

3. "Brain Connectivity Study Reveals Striking Differences Between Men and Women," Penn Medicine news release, December 2, 2013, http://www.uphs.upenn.edu/news/News_Releases/2013/12/verma/.

4. Emerson Eggerichs, *Love and Respect* (Nashville: Thomas Nelson, 2004).

5. S. Carrere, K. T. Buehlman, J. Gottman, J. A. Coan, and L. Ruckstuhl, "Predicting Marital Stability and Divorce in Newlywed Couples," *Journal of Family Psychology* 14, no. 1 (2000): 42–58.

Chapter 5: Living Under the Cloud of Negativity

1. John M. Gottman, *What Predicts Divorce?* (Hillsdale, NJ: Erlbaum, 1994).

2. John Gottman and Nan Silver, *The Seven Principles for Making Marriage Work* (New York: Crown, 1999).

3. D. K. Orthner, "Patterns of Leisure and Marital Satisfaction Over the Marital Career," *Journal of Marriage and the Family* 37 (1975): 91–102.

4. John M. Gottman and Robert W. Levinson, "Marital Processes Predictive of Later Dissolution: Behavior, Physiology and Health," *Journal of Personality and Social Psychology* 63 (2002): 221–33.

5. Barbara L. Fredrickson and M. F. Losada, "Positive Affect and the Complex Dynamics of Human Flourishing," *American Psychologist* 60 (2005): 678–86.

6. Ibid.

7. Gary Lewandowski, "Promoting Positive Emotions Following Relationship Dissolution Through Writing," *The Journal of Positive Psychology* 4, no. 1 (2009): 21–31.

Chapter 6: A Clash of Styles

1. Joyce A. Baptist, David E. Thompson, Aaron M. Norton, Nathan R. Hardy, and Chelsea D. Link, "The Effects of the Intergenerational Transmission of Family Emotional Processes on Conflict Styles: The Moderating Role of Attachment," *American Journal of Family Therapy* 40, no. 1 (2012): 56–73.

2. Kim Bartholomew and Leonard Horowitz, "Attachment Styles Among Young Adults: A Test of a Four Category Model," *Journal of Personality and Social Psychology* 61 (1991): 226–44.

3. John M. Gottman, *The Marriage Clinic* (New York: W.W. Norton, 1999), 88–89.

4. Dean Busby and Thomas Holman, "Perceived Match or Mismatch on the Gottman Conflict Styles: Associations with Relationship Outcome Variables," *Family Process* 48, no. 4 (2009): 531–45.

Chapter 8: All in the Family

1. S. L. Mikucki-Enyart, "Parent-in-Law Privacy Management: An Examination of the Links Among Relational Uncertainty, Topic Avoidance, In-Group Status, and In-Law Satisfaction," *Journal of Family Communication* 11 (2011): 237–63.

Notes

Chapter 9: Parenting, Divorce, and Blended Families

1. S. Shellenbarger, "Ambitious Parents, Mellow Children," *Wall Street Journal Online*, October 9, 2011, http://online.wsj.com/news/articles/SB100014240529702044 79504576638950410953960.
2. D. Baumrind, "Child-care Practices Anteceding Three Patterns of Preschool Behavior," *Genetic Psychology Monographs* 75 (1967): 43–88.
3. Ohio State University, "More Siblings Means Less Chance of Divorce As Adult," *ScienceDaily*, August 13, 2013, http://www.sciencedaily.com/releases/2013/08/130813101824.htm.
4. C. J. Tucker, D. Finkelhor, H. Turner, and A. Shattuck, "Association of Sibling Aggression with Child and Adolescent Mental Health," *The Journal of Pediatrics* (2013): 2012–3801.
5. J. H. Grych, F. D. Fincham, E. N. Jouriles, and R. McDonald, "Interparental Conflict and Child Adjustment: Testing the Mediational Role of Appraisals in the Cognitive-Contextual Framework," *Child Development* 71, no. 6 (200): 1648–61.
6. J. Folberg, A. L. Milne, and P. Salem, *Divorce and Family Mediation: Models, Techniques and Applications* (New York: Guildford Press, 2004).
7. Stanley S. Clawar and Brynne V. Rivlin, "Children Held Hostage: Dealing with Programmed and Brainwashed Children," *American Bar Association Section of Family Law* (1991): 180.

Chapter 10: Sex, Affection, and Conflict

1. Emily Brontë, http://thinkexist.com/quotes/emily_bronte/.
2. Transcript for "Helen Fisher Tells Us Why We Love, Cheat," TED Talk, December 17, 2008.
3. Ibid.
4. Helen Fisher, "The Realities of Love at First Sight," *O, The Oprah Magazine*, November 2009, http://www.oprah.com/relationships/Love-at-First-Sight-Helen-Fisher-Love-Column#ixzz2g65Uzvs9.
5. Michael R. Liebowitz, *The Chemistry of Love* (Boston: Little, Brown, and Co., 1983).
6. D. Furlow, "The Smell of Love," *Psychology Today*, March 1, 1996, http://www.psychologytoday.com/articles/200910/the-smell-love?page=2.
7. Claus Wedekind and Sandra Furi, "Body Odour Preferences in Men and Women: Do They Aim for Specific MHC Combinations or Simply Heterozygosity?" *Proc Biol Science* 264 (1997): 1471–79.
8. Michele Weiner-Davis, *The Sex-Starved Marriage* (New York: Simon and Schuster, 2004).
9. Daniel Amen, "Understand What Sex Does to Your Brain," *Men's Health*, http://www.menshealth.com/mhlists/understanding_sex_and_the_brain/Why_Her_Orgasms_are_Like_Paxil.php.
10. W. D. Johnson, "What Is the Difference Between Falling in Love and Physical Attraction?" December 13, 2013, http://www.ehow.com/info_8622015_difference-falling-love-physical-attraction.html#ixzz2fwLWCzc2.
11. K. J. Prager, *The Psychology of Intimacy* (New York: Guilford Press, 1995).

Notes

12. K. J. Prager and D. Buhrmester, "Intimacy and Need Fulfillment in Couple Relationships," *Journal of Social and Personal Relationships* 15 (1998): 435–69.

13. R. L. Scott and J. V. Cordova, "The Influence of Adult Attachment Styles on the Association Between Marital Adjustment and Depressive Symptoms," *Journal of Family Psychology* 2 (June 16, 2002): 199–208.

14. Gary Chapman, *The Five Love Languages: The Secret to Love That Lasts* (Chicago: Moody, 2009).

15. Shaunti Feldhahn, *For Women Only: What You Need to Know About the Inner Lives of Men* (Portland: Multnomah, 2004). Shaunti Feldhahn and Jeff Feldhahn, *For Men Only: A Straightforward Guide to the Inner Lives of Women* (Portland: Multnomah, 2006).

16. Helen Fisher, "The Realities of Love at First Sight," *O, The Oprah Magazine*, November 2009, http://www.oprah.com/relationships/Love-at-First-Sight-Helen-Fisher-Love-Column#ixzz2g65Uzvs9.

17. Helen Fisher, Arthur Aron, Debra Mashek, Haifang Li, and Lucy L. Brown, "Defining the Brain Systems of Lust, Romantic Attraction, and Attachment," *Archives of Sexual Behavior* 31, no. 5 (2002): 413–19.

18. Doug Eshelman, "Men View Half-Naked Women as Objects, Study Finds," *The Daily Prinstonian*, February 2009, http://www.sott.net/article/176636–Men-view-half-naked-women-as-objects-study-finds.

19. Anahad O'Conner, "In Sex, Brain Studies Show, 'la Différence' Still Holds," *New York Times*, March 16, 2004, http://www.nytimes.com/2004/03/16/health/in-sex-brain-studies-show-la-difference-still-holds.html?src=pm.

20. Joshua Scott, "Is Porn Harmful?" *Men's Health*, October 16, 2013, http://www.menshealth.com/sex-women/porn-debate/page/3.

21. J. D. Atwood and L. Schwartz, "Cybersex: The New Affair Treatment Considerations," *Journal of Couple and Relationship Therapy* 1, no. 3 (2002): 37.

22. Anthony Neal, "Journalist Spent a Month on Ashley Madison and Was Pleasantly Surprised by How Nice It Was," ashleymadison.com, December 13, 2013, https://www.ashleymadison.com/blog/journalist-spent-a-month-on-ashley-madison-and-was-pleasantly-surprised-by-how-nice-it-was/.

23. Lindsay Shugeman, "Percentage of Married Couples Who Cheat," Catalogs.com, http://www.catalogs.com/info/relationships/percentage-of-married-couples-who-cheat-on-each-ot.html.

24. "Facebook the Reason for Increase in Divorces?" facebookcheating.com, February 3, 2010, http://facebookcheating.com/archives/facebook-divorce-rise/.

25. "Does Facebook Wreck Marriages?" *Wall Street Journal*, May 21, 2012, http://blogs.marketwatch.com/realtimeadvice/2012/05/21/does-facebook-wreck-marriages/.

26. "What Actions Represent an On-line Affair?" facebookcheating.com, July 13, 2010, http://facebookcheating.com/archives/category/facebook-flirting/.

27. T. Shackelford, A. Besser, and A. Goetz, "Personality, Marital Satisfaction, and Probability of Marital Infidelity," *Journal of Individual Differences Research* 6, no. 1 (2008): 13–25.

Chapter 11: Dealing with Difficult People

1. "IN RE: Eben Gossage," August 14, 2000, http://caselaw.findlaw.com/ca -supreme-court/1130766.html.

Chapter 12: Anger and Resentment

1. "Alveda King: Grieved Over Strife Surrounding Zimmerman Verdict," July 15, 2013, Angel Pictures & Publicity press release.
2. R. Sapolsky, *Why Zebras Don't Get Ulcers: An Updated Guide to Stress, Stress-Related Diseases, and Coping* (New York: W. H. Freeman, 1998).
3. Theodore Rubin, *The Angry Book* (Ontario: Touchstone, 1998).
4. Redford Williams, *Anger Kills: Seventeen Strategies for Controlling the Hostility That Can Harm Your Health* (New York: Harper, 1994).

Chapter 13: Forgiveness

1. Brian Dakss, "Killer Drunk Driver Tries to Atone," February 3, 2005, CBS news, http://www.cbsnews.com/news/killer-drunk-driver-tries-to-atone/. And Debbie McLeland, *The Forgiveness Project*, March 29, 2010, http://theforgiveness project.com/stories/debbie-mcleland-usa/#prettyPhoto.
2. Eric Adelson, "Michael Vick Helps Clean Up Riley Cooper's Mess," *Yahoo Sports*, August 1, 2013, http://sports.yahoo.com/news/nfl--michael-vick-helping -to-clean-up-riley-cooper-s-mess-193236048.html.
3. "What Does the Research Say?" *Release! The Healing Power of Forgiveness*, http://releasenow.org/theresearch.
4. Joan Tupponce, "A Divine Test," *Richmond* magazine, January 30, 2009, http://www.richmondmagazine.com/articles/a-divine-test-01-13-2009.html.

Chapter 14: We Can Work It Out

1. "Divorce Statistics and Divorce Rate in the USA," http://www.divorcestatistics .info/divorce-statistics-and-divorce-rate-in-the-usa.html.

Dr. Linda Mintle is a national speaker and bestselling author of over fifteen books on relationships and mental health. She is the Chair, Behavioral Health, College of Osteopathic Medicine at Liberty University. Dr. Mintle appears regularly on national broadcasts and is a national news contributor in mental health. In addition, she hosts her own BeliefNet blog, *Doing Life Together*. Find out more about Dr. Linda Mintle at www.drlindamintle.com, Facebook (Dr. Linda Mintle, Author and Speaker), and Twitter (@drlindahelps).

FOLLOW

Dr. Linda Mintle

Therapist, Professor, Author, & Speaker

Visit drlindamintle.com

SIGN UP FOR DR. MINTLE'S

- bimonthly enewsletter,
- read her blog,
- and more.

 @drlindahelps